SO THE HEFFNERS LEFT McCOMB

Civil Rights in Mississippi
Trent Brown, General Editor

SO THE HEFFNERS LEFT McCOMB

HODDING CARTER II

Introduction by Trent Brown

UNIVERSITY PRESS OF MISSISSIPPI / JACKSON

www.upress.state.ms.us

The University Press of Mississippi is a member of the Association of American University Presses.

∞

Library of Congress Cataloging-in-Publication Data

Names: Carter, Hodding, 1907–1972, author.
Title: So the Heffners left McComb / Hodding Carter II.
Description: Jackson, MS : University Press of Mississippi, [2015] | Series: Civil rights in Mississippi | Originally published: 1965.
Identifiers: LCCN 2015041907 (print) | LCCN 2015042201 (ebook) | ISBN 9781496807489 (cloth : alk. paper) | ISBN 9781496807472 (pbk. : alk. paper) | ISBN 9781496807496 (ebook)
Subjects: LCSH: Heffner family. | Race discrimination—Mississippi—McComb. | Heffner, Albert W., Jr. | Heffner, Mary Alva. | Violence—Mississippi—McComb. | Harassment—Mississippi—McComb. | Civil rights movements—Mississippi—McComb. | African Americans—Civil rights—Mississippi—McComb. | McComb (Miss.)—Race relations. | McComb (Miss.)—Biography.
Classification: LCC F349.M16 C3 2015 (print) | LCC F349.M16 (ebook) | DDC 323.1196/073076223—dc23
LC record available at http://lccn.loc.gov/2015041907

British Library Cataloging-in-Publication Data available

reinforced by a neighbor's grant
FIGURE FOUNDATION

INTRODUCTION

Trent Brown, 2016

It is clearly not easy for man to give up the satisfaction of this
inclination to aggression. They do not feel comfortable without
it. The advantage which a comparatively small cultural group
offers of allowing this instinct an outlet in the form of hostility
against intruders is not to be despised. It is always possible to
bind together a considerable number of people in love, so long
as there are other people left over to receive the manifestations
of their aggressiveness.

FREUD—Civilization and Its Discontents

On Saturday, September 5, 1964, the Labor Day weekend,
the family of Albert W. "Red" Heffner Jr. left their house
at 202 Shannon Drive in McComb, Mississippi, where they
had lived for ten years. They never returned to the town.
On July 17 of that summer, they made a decision that would
within a few weeks cost them their home, Red's job, the
friends they thought they had made in the small southwest
Mississippi city, and their peace of mind. "We've had it,"
Red's wife Mary Alva ("Malva") told a reporter after they

left. "You'll never know the hell that was in our hearts."[1] In the eyes of their neighbors, their unforgivable sin was to have spoken on several occasions with civil rights workers in town and finally to have invited two of them to their house for conversation. Both of the civil rights workers, Rev. Don McCord and Dennis Sweeney, were white, although that did not seem to lessen the shock of the Heffners' action to the town. The evening of Friday, July 17, as the Heffners, McCord, and Sweeney discussed the summer's voter registration project in McComb, the Heffners became suddenly aware that their neighbors and others were and had been observing them. The telephone at their house rang, and an unidentified caller asked for Dennis Sweeney.[2] "How is the civil rights work going?" a woman's voice asked. After realizing the potentially dangerous nature of the call, Sweeney hung up the telephone. Later that evening, cars began circling the Heffners' block.

Over the next weeks, the anonymous phone calls continued, becoming increasingly vulgar and threatening. Malva recalled that they eventually received more than three hundred harassing calls. People in the neighborhood, if not active participants in the intimidation campaign against them, were certainly aware of the dangers the Heffners faced. One afternoon a four-year-old boy asked Mrs. Heffner, "When is your house going to be bombed?" a reasonable question considering the level of violence in the town that summer. Red Heffner had seen his role only as a possible line of communication between respectable white McComb and the civil rights workers. Even though he informed police chief George Guy, a man he considered to be his friend, of his actions and attempted to explain his reasoning to people in town he thought would surely understand his desire to help keep matters calm that summer, the community turned with viciousness on the family, who were "despised, suspected, ostracized, and economically crippled."[3]

The fall of the Heffners from the community's grace was swift and complete. Their story demonstrates the power of fear, conformity, community pressure, and threats of retaliation of many sorts that silenced so many white Mississippians against the violence of the summer of 1964 as well as during the longer period of the civil rights movement in the state during the 1950s and 1960s. *So the Heffners Left McComb* is journalist Hodding Carter II's succinct account of the events that led to the Heffners' downfall and flight from their home.[4] It is not a history of the broader civil rights movement in the city or of the voter registration campaign that triggered a wave of violence in McComb that summer. It concentrates instead on the background of the Heffners, their immediate actions in the early summer of 1964, and the campaign of intimidation that drove them from their hometown. Even on those terms, it is not an account of the full community's thoughts and actions. Black McComb figures very little in Carter's account, as he admits. The best role he could imagine for them in a telling of the community's story is as a "shadowy, contrapuntal chorus" (10), a metaphor that says much about the limits in those days even of a sympathetic white Mississippian such as Carter. The students and other volunteers who came for the Mississippi Freedom Summer, Carter sets down as engaged in an "idealist if foolhardy project" (10). Their plans, voices, and fates receive little attention here. No, the book is by design an account of white McComb and its rejection of the Heffners.

It is easy to see what Carter omitted, some things by design and others because he wrote the account immediately after the events he recounts. But by showing how acutely community pressure could turn on and drive away one previously respected white family during the most intense period of the civil rights movement in Mississippi, Carter's book stands as an important but largely neglected document.

Early histories of the civil rights movement, as well as many popular accounts, focus on leaders like Martin Luther King Jr., opponents such as George Wallace, or action or inaction at the national level by Congress or Presidents Kennedy or Johnson. More recent scholarly work generally concentrates on local people, either activists or opponents of reform.[5] Carter's book, on the other hand, features a family that never chose to make a stand on the principles of the struggle in that time and place, yet were deliberately and systematically punished and driven into exile for what white McComb perceived as a most serious breach of the racial solidarity upon which the community rested and depended. Like most of their white middle-class peers in McComb, the Heffners felt invested in their community, church, and other local institutions. That investment led them to seek a way of understanding what was happening locally as national attention and grassroots pressure intensified on what most whites called without sarcasm the Mississippi Way of Life. The Heffners felt that the voter registration campaign in the state that summer and the violent white response to it represented something new and potentially disruptive to their community, and hoped through mediation or at least communication to end the violence that had begun in McComb as soon as the first "outsiders" had come to town. The longer tradition of violence against local blacks, on the other hand, seemed never to have excited much attention from Red Heffner. That violence was certainly less visible or somehow simply less troubling even to moderate white McComb, if only because it did not figure so prominently in the local or national press or in conversations with other community leaders and respectable people. Nor, it should be noted, did that longer pattern of violence against black McComb feature a summer dynamiting terrorist campaign, as happened in 1964.

How could the Heffners become outcasts so quickly in the eyes of a community that had previously welcomed them? The Heffners, practically anyone in McComb would have said, were respectable people; indeed, they were respected rather than simply respectable. Malva Heffner's first husband, Bob Nave, was killed in the Battle of the Bulge. Jan Nave, twenty-one, her daughter and his, was a student at the Mississippi State College for Women and was completing her year as Miss Mississippi, in an era when the South followed such pageants with a vengeance. Their daughter Carla, seventeen, was perhaps less conventionally studious than her sister, but was a serious reader and enjoyed writing. Hodding Carter notes that even before the summer, she had a "preoccupation with civil rights" (16). Given to outspokenness, as was her father, Carla was generally popular at McComb High School, where she was a member of the Class of 1965. Both Malva and Red had attended Ole Miss. Red had been honored by the Lincoln National Life insurance company for which he worked, and McComb civic organizations recognized him as an outstanding young man. They were active in their local Episcopal congregation, the Church of the Redeemer, one of the few affiliations that did differentiate them from their peers in the overwhelmingly Baptist and Methodist city. In short, though, they were strivers—community-oriented people who fit in. They were the sort who provided "leadership" in business, town government, and churches throughout the region. In writing the story of their exile, Hodding Carter told of a family with whom he certainly identified—moderate, thoughtful, and interested in their community, but at the same time accepting of segregation and other "realities" of the southern situation, while deploring vulgar or violent behavior in its defense. The Heffners were not, in other words, outsiders (until they seemed to become so that summer) or troublemakers who found the trouble for which they came looking, as many white southerners said of that summer's civil rights workers. Shortly after they left McComb, Malva Heffner told a reporter, "If it could happen to us, it could happen to anyone." Carter's book is usefully viewed as a detailed, convincing exposition of that hypothesis.

One of the safest generalizations to make about McComb, Mississippi, is that few cities in the state experienced such a sustained, intense period of violence during the civil rights movement of the 1960s, and that few places of comparable violent resistance in the entire South have until very recently made less of an effort to understand, reflect upon, or come to terms with that fact. As is true throughout most of the state, there are no statues in McComb to commemorate the struggles of the 1960s, but during the Heffners' years in town, there were no statues to earlier wars, either. McComb was a railroad town, founded after the Civil War. There were no Faulknerian memories, in marble or otherwise, that might serve as markers of a Confederate past, white Redemption, or anything else that might indicate a reserve of civil memory upon which a scene like the 1960s might have played out as one of those periodic challenges that rises, is dealt with, and then joins in the larger remembered history of order triumphing over chaos.

The lack of official public commemoration and discussion of the civil rights movement is not because, as in nearby Brookhaven, for instance, nothing of great value from the pre-1970 period seems to have been lost by local whites. That is to say, the lack of statues and other memorials is not because the years marked no significant events or changes. Indeed, elective politics, the schools, and other similar areas of contestation have certainly accommodated black power—and that is a term that needs careful qualification in this context—in ways that other communities in the state simply have not done as thoroughly or without a white retreat from the public schools or from the geographical boundaries of the community itself, as in Jackson, the state capital. Put simply, the McComb schools and McComb politics became areas of active black participation and authority in the 1980s and 1990s without generating the kind of white retreat that marks the dreadfully depressed communities of the Delta or the financially strapped capital city of Jackson. But this is not to say that McComb is a model for reconciliation or accommodation or a useful working arrangement between whites and blacks, for the circumstances that have caused the disappearance of the memory of the Heffners as well as a general amnesia (in the white public, at least) of those years, is contingent and specific, just as were the circumstances that led white McComb to drive away the Heffners in 1964.

McComb's Carroll Oaks subdivision, where the Heffners bought a new house in 1954, was initially indistinguishable from many thousands of other collections of moderately prosperous ranch-style houses built in the United States during the 1950s and 1960s. Such houses were the ones in which World War II–era veterans raised their families and worked at white-collar or professional jobs like the one that Red Heffner had selling insurance policies in those long-ago days of middle-class prosperity and one-income families. In the mid-1960s, Carroll Oaks seemed new and fashionable and in mid-century style, and bore little resemblance to the solid Victorians, occasional Spanish Colonial, tidy bungalows, and other interesting architectural styles to be found in the old neighborhoods of west and central McComb, especially those around and off of centrally located Delaware Avenue. But while the subdivision was nouveau, it was not riche, at least not in any way that spoke meaningfully of white social class tensions. White McComb's modest homes were not conspicuously divided from those of the more prosperous white professionals and older families by any striking or well-known boundaries. Such proximity, which meant that white children of the town spent their school years together, almost certainly led to a sense of community and pride in the neat little town that went beyond the usual rhetoric of civic boosterism. The closest thing to a white social divide in the town was "East McComb," where modest houses and warehouses and small business and light industry existed side-by-side with railroad workers and their families.

For McComb was a railroad town, in ways that were remembered and not remembered in the 1960s. But that origin and economic definition meant a great deal to the town's history. McComb lies just to the west of what was in the late-nineteenth century a rich and tremendous belt of white pine timber. The extraction of that timber provided an important, but not a determinative role in the economy of the town. And its location, in any case, was not determined solely by proximity to that natural resource. One of the local pieces of lore that was remembered and is still circulated was that McComb City was located one hundred miles above New Orleans as the site of the repair shops for the southern end of the great Illinois Central railroad line. And those shops were in fact a great, stable, unionized employer of white and black Pike Countians for decades. Locals said that railroad magnate Henry McComb wanted his workers protected from the fleshpots of New Orleans, the southern terminus of the line. In unofficial and semi-official tellings, few people have noted that the one-hundred-mile distance also coincided, not coincidentally, with union regulations for the relief of train crews. Union stories were not ones that most New South communities, even progressive ones, typically included among their origin myths. Striking but perhaps not surprising in this context is that few McComb residents recalled that the community had a short but sharp period of railroad labor violence during the national railroad strike of 1911, with the violence coming through company strikebreakers, supplemented by troops called out by the governor.[6] By the time of the war, which here always meant World War II, stories of white class division were or at least seemed to be forgotten, especially when black McComb showed signs of resistance to disfranchisement and other manifestations of Jim Crow in the 1950s and especially the 1960s.

By the 1960s, McComb did in fact have a tradition of black civil rights activism that still seeks full treatment by historians. In Pike County and in neighboring Amite County, blacks long had quietly (as far as most whites knew) worked to accumulate such property and land as they could, operate small businesses such as hotels and restaurants and venues for black performing artists, and challenge their status in the face of constant white resistance and always the threat of violence. McComb never witnessed the familiar civil rights–era drama of black citizens running the hostile gauntlet of a white crowd to a centrally located courthouse fronted by a Confederate monument. For McComb was not the seat of Pike County; Magnolia was, and so there was the courthouse. Black voter registration activities, however, were certainly no secret to the sheriff or to the political and business powers of McComb, but the bulk of white McComb's citizens simply did not witness voter registration activities, pickets, and other visible forms of resistance, let alone "outside agitators," until the 1960s. It was perhaps easy there, as it was in many other Mississippi communities, for whites to imagine that black McComb was basically content with its lot.

As Hodding Carter notes, McComb in the summer of 1964 was aware of several basic facts, as they saw it. The state and the community were preparing for an invasion, as the Jackson newspapers insisted on calling it, of civil rights activists, who were coming to work on the Summer Project, as the Congress of Federated Organizations (COFO) initially referred to the Freedom Summer campaign. Editor Oliver Emmerich's McComb *Enterprise-Journal* began to write about the summer plans early in 1964, although not in a way that seemed alarmist by Mississippi standards, which is perhaps only to say that he did not suggest that the summer would bring Armageddon, with the hints for white McComb to gird their loins for battle.[7] So white McComb was prepared in one sense, but not tempered by the stronger counsels about moderation and the rule of law the Emmerich delivered later in the autumn of 1964, after the Heffners were gone and the bombings and other massive violence had largely ceased. McComb was prepared in the sense of having time to reflect upon the meaning that the summer might hold and what they might be able to do about it. Scholars have noted that the Mississippi Ku Klux Klan was in the 1950s and early 1960s less formally organized than similar organizations in other states. State authority and local white opinion served perhaps as a sufficient check on black ambitions in those days. For McComb, as in other parts of the state, certainly by the mid-1960s that situation had changed as the civil rights movement became more active and visible. Vigilante organizations organized under the auspices of the Klan were vocal, armed with formidable stocks of dynamite, and complemented by the public propaganda and oratory of less outlaw-seeming organizations such as the Americans for the Preservation of the White Race. White McComb, then, was forewarned, forearmed, and unusually prepared by their successful repulse of "agitators" such as Robert Moses and others who had come to town in 1961 to work for voter registration, an event that was largely absent from local newspaper commentary in 1964, but had surely taught something to both whites and blacks in the community about what to expect that summer.

C. C. Bryant, local McComb businessman and civil rights activist, recalled that the city was in 1964 "a hell on earth," a phrase now inscribed on the Freedom Trail monument (placed in July, 2014), with which the state now commemorates his work that summer and in earlier years. By almost any measure, the city experienced some of the most sustained violence of any southern town or city of any size. While Oxford, Philadelphia, and Jackson might figure more largely in histories and popular narratives of the civil rights era in Mississippi, McComb may be relatively neglected only because of the absence (at least in the eyes of Hollywood and many documentary filmmakers) of a singular figure like James Meredith around which to build a story, or the presence of martyrs such as the three Philadelphia lynching victims. Given the amount of bombing and shooting in the county in 1964, however, it is not for lack of trying that violent men in McComb failed to kill people.

Indeed, the level of visible, property-damaging violence became so great and so nationally (if briefly) notorious that rumors swept through town that President Lyndon Johnson was preparing to declare martial law in McComb. At that point, whether or not those rumors ever proved to have much foundation, the *Enterprise Journal* began to call for order, which, as we have been reminded again in recent years, is not precisely the same thing as arguing that homicidal bombers should receive justice. Finally, in November the newspaper ran a "Statement of Principles," drafted by a committee of businessmen and signed by more than 650 (white) city residents, many of them doctors, dentists, business owners, and members of the town's most noted families. Many of the points spelled out seem basic: all arrests should be for legitimate reasons, a statement which attests to the broad authority law enforcement officers in the period possessed. Activists were liable not only to trumped-up arrests on specious charges, but also for violating statutes against disturbing the peace, distributing leaflets, and serving food without a license, the latter used against the summer's Freedom Houses. Another provision of the statement suggested that public officeholders should not be members of subversive organizations (such as the Ku Klux Klan). The statement is little more than that: a statement, since it did not call for nor did it lead to any structural changes, let alone clear amelioration of many black residents' basic grievances. Nor did it end the bombing, as some people in the city still claim. The bombing had by that time largely petered out, the fall elections had been held, and the summer volunteers had left. Instead, the statement is perhaps best understood as a commentary on the possibilities that white McComb believed in during that summer. A call for an end to future recourse to extralegal, organized violence came late, and came only in the company of a large enough and prominent enough group to ensure that no one seemed conspicuous by inclusion. Two of my grandparents signed (one was a grocer); two of them did not (one of them owned a beauty shop on Delaware Avenue, where I lived as a child). Few of the signers spoke publicly about their decision to endorse the statement; the dissenters did not, either.

The "Statement of Principles" published in November reveals the caution with which the "respectable" people of the town approached the summer's violence. The fact that the summer project was over before the statement was published also speaks to the alleged power of the people of the city to "do something." If these doctors, businessmen, and other professionals, could not, who could? If they would not, does the statement mean anything? In their partial defense, it is always easier to demand of the past that people should "do something" than it is to consider how confusing and daunting a social revolution can appear when one is living through it. In any case, the McComb Statement commits a logical error as common in our time as in theirs: the fallacy of the false middle. The signatories called on "extremists of both sides" to calm down and cool off, a position that in another place in the South, Martin Luther King had memorably demolished in the "Letter from Birmingham Jail." The closest that the statement comes to revealing deep, troubling injustice within the community is the provision that holders of offices of public trust (such as sheriff's deputies and police officers) ought not be members of groups identified by national authorities as subversive organizations. Otherwise, the statement reveals little about the substantive, long-term grievances that the black people of McComb faced before the summer project came and ended. The statement was published after all but a few of the summer workers had left Mississippi. The Atlantic City Democratic convention in August had failed to produce a seating of the Mississippi Freedom Democratic Party delegation, one of the goals of many of the organizers of Freedom Summer. The presidential election had occurred, with Republican candidate Barry Goldwater receiving over 90 percent of the votes counted officially in McComb. And the Heffners had left McComb, and Mississippi as well.

By the summer of 1964 most residents of McComb, especially those who signed the statement, no longer believed that massive resistance of the Klan type could keep matters settled for good. But the cost of speaking out still carried risks of clan ostracism, if not overt violence. Red Heffner was braver than the average person, and perhaps more pugnacious, too. Yet at bottom he understood that he was the sole source of income for his wife and two daughters. As an insurance salesman, he had to be careful of the facts that neither his goods nor his services were irreplaceable. The appearance of unorthodoxy, even the modest act of speaking with white civil rights workers in his home, signaled to his neighbors that Red's community bona fides were essentially discredited. Those who circled his house in automobiles, spoke obscenities over the telephone, and poisoned his dog remained anonymous, although certainly not all were unknown to the Heffners. Others, such as the landlord who evicted Red Heffner from his office space, did not act in the darkness, but it is at least understandable that in a season of bombings, a man might have to be careful about the people to whom he rented. This hesitancy of white McComb to denounce a level of bombing that one might today call domestic terrorism suggests one of the real and lasting values of Carter's book.

Red Heffner's confidence that he was a respected member of the community is indicated by his initial belief in the summer of 1964 that he and prominent people in McComb had not only an interest in tamping down violence in the community, but also that they had the ability to do so. At least, presumed Heffner, his efforts might be seen, by some at least, as potentially useful. Hodding Carter points out that Heffner consulted with McComb police chief George Guy before he invited the civil rights workers to his home, a form of insurance that was badly undercut when Guy later refuted Heffner's public account of that consultation. Hodding Carter calls Chief Guy a "conscientious and competent police officer" (40). But one must note also that Guy, the man to whom Heffner looked for support when the town began to turn against him, admitted years later that he was the head of the local branch of the Americans for the Preservation of the White Race. Historian Joseph Crespino points out that at the 1967 Mississippi State Fair that organization "sold booklets . . . that contained explicit diagrams on how to construct homemade bombs."[8]

The Heffners were both economically and socially vulnerable at a time when the broader white community's senses of threat and outrage were unusually heightened by press coverage and by a handful of white "outsiders" in the community, the summer volunteers. What happened to the Heffners? They were not murdered, beaten, or bombed or burned out, although the family well knew that could have been the next step in the campaign. Instead, they joined the ranks of voluntary white exiles from the Jim Crow order that probably peaked in the state before they left; the phenomenon is less visible and less studied than the black migration. The Heffners' fate seems different too from that of James Silver or Ed King or other white Mississippians who decided to stand against the mad storm by withstanding its public scorn as long as they could after taking action they knew would alienate them from the white community. Those more famous exiles have drawn a scholarly attention that, while merited, probably has obscured other, quieter departures.

Why did no one speak out to reassure the white community that the Heffners were not a threat to them? Were there no old McComb families whose reputation could shield an eccentric, within the family or not, against charges of racial heterodoxy? The "best people" in the town were doctors, attorneys, and other professionals—there was nothing on the order of a Sartoris family here, with a pedigree that extended back well in the nineteenth century; the town was too new for that. But many families were admired, and many of them for good reasons, such as a devotion to the arts, youth sports or Boy Scouts, or other forms of volunteerism, as well as efforts at community economic development. Red Heffner and his family had not quite moved into that orbit, nor likely would have done, even if they had stayed in McComb for more years. His trade as an insurance salesman made him particularly vulnerable to the vicissitudes of the reputation of the agent. And Red Heffner in 1964 already had a reputation for speaking his mind, a trait that probably seemed more significant when the summer wore on. When he lost his office space and his reputation, there seemed little possibility that the family could afford to stay in town, literally or figuratively. No multigenerational ties there existed to cushion the Heffner family from the blow. So they left McComb.

McComb's summer of 1964 took place within the broader context of the Mississippi Project, an effort coordinated by COFO, a coalition of civil rights groups, to register black voters, to provide them access to civic and other basic forms of education, and generally to call national attention to conditions in the state regarded (along perhaps with Alabama) as most likely to offer recalcitrant and violent resistance to efforts for black civil rights, whether their efforts came from the courts, the national government, or local activism. From the Emmett Till slaying through the assassination of Medgar Evers, Mississippi had provided evidence of the price that it was willing to exact to maintain the Jim Crow order in the state. The national civil rights organizations operating under the COFO umbrella were in 1963 and 1964 still officially committed to nonviolence, but they were also committed to the idea that Mississippi and other southern states would yield nothing without pressure and visibility, a strategy that set them at odds with the national NAACP, as well as black middle-class and professional Mississippians who believed that strife might endanger their position both within the black community and their dealings with local whites, who recognized and indeed helped to provide their status as respectable leaders.

The Mississippi Project brought more than a thousand students and other volunteers to the state to work with a small number of established civil rights activists and local people to assist black Mississippians in attempting to claim their basic civil rights. The campaign's organizers screened college applicants to attempt to weed out conscious martyrs, the potentially violent, and the immature. The summer volunteers spent weeks living with black families, canvassing for voter registration applicants, educating young and old black Mississippians in the rudiments of civil rights, literature, history, and the arts; building freedom schools and libraries; handling correspondence, coordinating telephone calls, stuffing envelopes, waiting for scanty weekly checks that always seemed a bit delayed and insufficient; and generally enduring a hostile reception from whites that sometimes provided but always loomed with the threat of violence. Given the state's high level of emotional and physical preparedness for the "invasion," it is probably due in great measure to the savvy and experience of local black Mississippians that more student volunteers were not seriously injured or killed.

Of the many ironies of Mississippi history, certainly a significant one is that the aims of the summer project—the "invasion" that led to the Heffners' exile—were relatively modest and, despite white fears to the contrary, not revolutionary. The project aimed not at a real redistribution of power and resources, but rather for modest beginnings of black political participation. Mississippi, with the largest percentage of black population in the nation, still had a black population of less than forty percent of the state's total. Only six percent of them were registered to vote at the beginning of that summer. With no Voting Rights Act yet in place, no federal sense of responsibility for the volunteers or the civil rights of black Mississippians, and no real mood for or tradition of open violent efforts by black Mississippians to change Mississippi laws or customs, white Mississippians had little possibility of seeing a real revolution come to the state that summer. They still held a monopoly on state-sanctioned force, and the laws of Mississippi still offered little protection to anyone that locally powerful people or violent vigilantes wished to punish. Just as important, perhaps, the bulk of the white volunteers who came to Mississippi still believed that America might work as the civics textbooks suggested that it should, or less cynically, that America was a society that could be called upon to listen to the better angels of its nature. Certainly most black Mississippians knew better than that. The summer of 1964 would prove an education for most of the volunteers as well as the Heffners.

By the time Hodding Carter II wrote his book on Mc-
Comb, he had earned a national reputation as a moderate
or even a progressive newspaper editor and writer.[9] Moderation and progressiveness always have been relative terms
when applied to white southerners, both within the region
and in a national context. Both labels seem generally more
trouble than they are worth, but as people in the 1960s and
later have insisted upon using the terms, it is just as well to
confront them, as long as one is clear about the uses and
the limits of such labels. Louisiana-born Carter made his
reputation as a newspaper editor, first in his native state and
after 1939, in Mississippi. Trained at the Columbia University School of Journalism after taking an undergraduate
degree at Bowdoin College, Carter returned to the South.
First working as a reporter in New Orleans, other Louisiana
cities, and briefly in Jackson, Mississippi, he then founded,
with his wife, the former Betty Werlein, the *Hammond*
(Louisiana) *Daily Courier*. The paper quickly developed a
reputation as a scourge of the Huey Long administration,
not a unique stand in the state, as the New Orleans newspapers had been largely critical of Long since his entry into
politics as a critic of the established gas, oil, and other mon-
ied interests in the state. Carter's criticism, however, rested
upon the rich and growing body of evidence that the King-
fish not only ran Louisiana as his fiefdom, which few doubted and many applauded, but that he used particularly venal,
corrupt, and violent means to hold power and to silence his
critics. For his forays into investigative journalism, Carter
defended both his paper and himself with strong language
and occasionally with larger caliber weapons, in the long tradition of the sometimes-raucous southern press.

Whether opposition to Huey Long was progressive or moderate or even conservative is somewhat pointless to ask. Brave it certainly was, and potentially dangerous, too. The Carters relocated to Greenville, Mississippi, a cosmopolitan town for its size, with a lively group of writers and thinkers such as the Percys and a young Shelby Foote. He founded the Greenville *Delta Democrat-Times*, a newspaper later edited by his son and then his grandson. Carter's newspaper was never deliberately provocative or quixotic in the manner of those edited by Hazel Brannon Smith in Mississippi or Harry Golden in North Carolina. But his paper was influential and it survived the displeasure of some of his readers and much of the state's political leadership; those latter qualities in themselves are worth noting, especially in the light of subsequent criticism of Carter's moderation by those who fault him for not staking out positions on African American rights more advanced than he took. After taking positions in advance of much public opinion, Carter won the 1946 Pulitzer Prize for editorials criticizing America's treatment of Japanese-American World War II veterans. And in the 1950s, he strongly denounced the Citizens' Council in the national press and in his own paper at a time when the organization enjoyed great and growing power in the state, and came to function almost as a branch of government. There was nothing meek or moderate about attacking the Citizens' Council, a native Delta growth, during the mid and late 1950s. Many among his readers were members or sympathizers of the Kiwanis Klan, as some called it, which certainly did as much as its redneck cousin in steeling the resolve of many white Mississippians to resist changes to their way of life.

It is perhaps in his growing role of native interpreter of the South to the nation that Carter is most vulnerable to charges that he represented a line of thinking that is now largely discredited. That counsel was patience with the white South as it was allowed time to work out its own solution to matters like school segregation and the larger claims of the emerging civil rights movement. By the mid-1960s, Carter's advice to be patient and wait for the South to reform its own soul and institutions seemed obsolete, if not worse, but Carter was not the only white southerner to be caught in that intellectual and moral trap. But two things must be said in Carter's defense: first, his moderation never seemed a cover for doing nothing; second, we have become little better in the last century in confronting the fierce urgency of now, as Martin Luther King put it. There were more discreditable stands in the white South in that era than suggesting that the region was not yet prepared for the kinds of sacrifices that reform demanded, and that the broader American nation showed itself no more ready than the Deep South to face.

Nowhere in Carter's book does he suggest that the Heffners themselves acted too hastily, or that their interests and rights would have been better served if McComb had simply been allowed to "cool off" for a spell so that hotheads "on both sides," as Carter, to his credit, never put it, could be persuaded to leave and allow the people of goodwill to work things out on their own terms and on their own timetable. Carter certainly did not set out to write the Heffner book as a refutation of moderation and gradualism, although that is perhaps one of the clearest messages to emerge from its pages. If people like the Heffners could not so much as seek to hear what white civil rights workers, including a clergyman, had to say for themselves, what a mockery it is to suggest that the South in due time might awaken to a sense of moderation and responsibility. If white Mississippians with a record of respectability such as that of the Heffners could so quickly be labeled an outsiders and traitors, what hope for anyone more legitimately considered an outsider or agitator? And if the moderate and professional classes of McComb showed so little power of resistance to violence, and indeed seem to have sanctioned the ostracism of the family, what must that say about the poverty of Atticus Finch-like heart-by-heart reform in the South of the 1960s? Historian Joseph Crespino has persuasively and provocatively explored what he calls the strange career of Atticus Finch.[10] The tragic career of Red Heffner, more than those of Atticus Finch, James Meredith, or even Medgar Evers, contains hard and neglected lessons, unsuited for generations of school children as they might be, about the limits of the individual heart and individual action in effecting change upon what Reinhold Neibuhr called moral man in immoral society. No one in McComb, black or white, could creditably believe that a handful of college-aged students attempting to work in tandem with nonviolent black local people could really have achieved an economic or political revolution.

But perhaps revolution is too strong a word for what white McComb dreaded, even in an era when the threat of communism was taken seriously in all manner of contexts. Change may be a better word for what white McComb resisted—change that might not be on their terms or lead to a way of life in which they believed. Otherwise, one's temptation might be too quickly to attribute the fate of the Heffners to simple racism or fear. And no doubt racism and fear were plentiful in Mississippi that summer. What, then, was really at stake, and why were the Heffners forced to leave McComb? If one were white in McComb in the 1950s and 1960s, during that long economic boom, life could seem basically good, and certainly better in economic terms than a childhood spent in rural Mississippi during the Depression. A desire for stability, order, and conformity were not unique to American southerners in those years. Take away the dynamite, the neighborhood watch society, and the power of the police to arrest disturbers of the peace (a term more apt than the Mississippi legislature knew), and down comes Eden. For people do not wish to be told, as white McComb citizens had been told in a variety of contexts for a long time, that the habits of their heart (and those habits can include hatred) were corrupt. No doubt many in Pike County thought that they hated outsiders, or liberals, or black people, but many too hated communism or sin or people who seemed to threaten their families and way of life, hatreds that they also believed to be ones that squared them with the gods that they trusted to preserve their way of life.

By Mississippi standards, Heffner was bold in calling for calm in the face of the prospect of the summer of 1964. That such a seemingly modest position was regarded as threatening by his neighbors makes more sense when one considers that in McComb, in preparation for what some claimed would be a campaign of rape and hooliganism, the sale "of small arms, ammunition, dynamite, and Ku Klux Klan memberships boomed," according to John Dittmer. In 1962, well before Freedom Summer began, Malva Heffner wrote a letter, not published, to the Jackson *Clarion-Ledger*, a newspaper rabidly opposed to any sort of modus vivendi with the civil rights movement. She called the newspaper and Governor Ross Barnett to task for not preparing the state for the changes that would inevitably come to the Jim Crow order and for not working to keep the state calm in the face of the storm that Heffner feared would come and that would threaten something more than race relations in the state. In the early summer of 1964, Red Heffner's conviction was that violence as a response to civil rights work was not only bad in itself, but that it posed dollars and cents danger to communities like McComb. By violence, one must note, Heffner meant such acts as bombings, assassinations, and other unmistakable outbursts—not necessarily the smaller and more pervasive acts of terror with which black Mississippians lived. Their other belief, soon badly contradicted by the fate of their family, maintained that the most effective tool against violence was the public stand and public statements against terror.

As late as July, Red Heffner wrote to a long-term acquaintance: "if the Citizen's Councils and the Legislator [sic] would 'just shut up' for a few weeks we could all go back to making a living." The man to whom he wrote was Erle Johnson Jr., the director of the Sovereignty Commission, a state agency that was by this point acting as an investigatory and propaganda agency, working to monitor and undermine civil rights efforts throughout the state. The letter is candid and revealing; Heffner perhaps did not know that it went into the file that the Sovereignty Commission had begun compiling on him. He described to Johnson an "effort" in McComb to persuade the local bar and medical associations and the

Chamber of Commerce to issue a statement (not a strong statement," he said) condemning the violence, especially as the New York press was providing coverage of events in Mississippi that summer, including McComb, a fact particularly frustrating, wrote Heffner, because the coverage happened "at a time when we are just on the verge of closing a Jim dandy industrial prospect." Heffner was certainly not in a position to benefit directly or to figure largely in the dealing necessary to bring a factory to the town, nor was he a man of a great deal of influence in any of the groups he believed ought to take a public stand against violence. Instead, he wrote and acted simply as a civic-minded man—one who deplored violence as not only bad for business and the reputation of the town, but also as one who saw it as the act of "the lowest form of coward." In the end, as it turned out, the Heffners were indeed victims of people who hid their faces from them, one way or another.

And what of McComb and the Heffners after the family was driven from town in the fall of 1964? The city's story is the easier one to tell. The bombings and other attempts at assassination and other violent suppression of the civil rights movement largely ended without federal or state intervention or any dramatic denouement. In the first few decades after Freedom Summer, when the violence was remembered at all by the white citizens in town, it was as a story of the responsible people of the town taking a stand and reclaiming the city from those violent men who wanted to make something of the town other than what it truly was. Those who had signed the *Enterprise-Journal*'s "Statement of Principles," as well as the paper's editor Oliver Emmerich, were remembered as people who poured balm on

troubled waters and turned out the extremists. This reassuring story seems somewhat short of the truth, but one
can understand why many white people in the town might
have wanted to think so. In the aftermath of the bombings, a
handful of men were arrested and tried for their part in that
summer's reign of terror. Most of them were working class,
with jobs as mechanics or for the Illinois Central Railroad;
one, though, was a troubled, criminally inclined son of one
of McComb's financial first families. At their trial, the men
received suspended or incredibly light punishments. Many
of these callow youth, one notes, were in their thirties, and it
ought to go without saying that such punishments to fit such
crimes reflected something other than current Mississippi
philosophy about the most effective ways to rehabilitate
youth. Indeed, the judge announced that the men had been
"unduly provoked" by agitators of low morals and hygiene.[11]

One explanation for the end of the violence in 1964 and
through the end of the decade is relatively simple: people
in town largely accepted that the Civil Rights Act of 1964
and the Voting Rights Act of 1965 would be enforced. Too,
part of the explanation is that the Freedom Summer campaign ended and most of the volunteers returned to college or work in other places and movements. There were
no more Freedom Houses, national press attention, or active, organized, nonindigenous freedom campaigns at work
in the city. Official opposition to black voter registration in
the county subsided, and black Pike Countians, along with
other Mississippians, began to influence elections as soon as
1968 and more so into the 1970s. And in 1970, the public
schools of McComb were racially integrated, as the Fifth
Circuit Court in New Orleans ordered an immediate end to

the dual school systems in the state. Without much incident, the people of the city, black and white, complied, although recalcitrant whites opened one of the segregation academies, this one called Parklane, that sprouted in many parts of the state when segregationists recognized that "never" had finally come. The school still operates, although its segregationist roots are no longer discussed in polite company. So, then, the whites of the county appear to have made the same accommodation with basic elements of the civil rights campaign—voting, school desegregation, the operation of certain Great Society programs and their successors—while not surrendering real economic power in the town. By the 1970s and 1980s, then, the most fundamental and common topic of political conversation for a generation—the necessity and determination of white Mississippians to preserve segregation as the foundation of their Way of Life—had passed out of open discourse. The civil rights movement itself did not dominate the headlines of the local newspaper in the 1970s, except as it played out in court cases at various levels and the enforcement of their decisions; it was often easy not to dwell on the fact that the summer campaign of 1964 had even occurred.

In recent years, however, McComb, has joined other Mississippi towns in beginning to commemorate the civil rights struggles of the 1960s. In cooperation with the Mississippi Department of Archives and History, signs in the city now mark physical landmarks and key participants in that era— C. C. Bryant's house and business, Aylene Quinn's restaurant and home, for example—and others are scheduled to join them. One can even take a driving tour of the city keyed to homes, churches, businesses, and other sites of significance to the black community's efforts to secure civil rights, including McComb's former black high school and the bus station that witnessed arrests and other violence. The years since 1970 have been hard on McComb's formerly active black business district. Little remains now to bear witness to the large number of black patrons who enjoyed its restaurants, lodging places, and music and other performance venues. To this date, however, neither official state or city remembrances of those years or less formal but perhaps more important black reunions and other commemorations have marked the house in the Carroll Oaks subdivision from which the Heffner family fled in the fall of 1964.

And what of the Heffners themselves? None of them ever returned to McComb, either to live or for any other reason. Red and Malva are both dead, and they died before it became fashionable or correct to offer apologies or any kind of recognition of their losses from that time. It is not easy to say what form such an apology might take, in any case, as they were not punished by arrest or any kind of official city action that might be rescinded or expunged from any record. Their persecution came at the hands of men and women who for the most part lived out their lives in the town respected or forgotten for what they did at that time or at least never called in any meaningful way to account for what they did. Red and Malva, especially Malva, expressed regret and sadness at their fate. Neither expressed hatred for McComb or for the people who terrorized or ostracized them. And neither, at the time, offered anything like an apology or recantation of their actions in attempting to understand and to communicate with the civil rights forces that were unfolding in their community during that summer. The sisters

Jan and Carla maintained the same sort of divergence over the years that they had shown during their adolescence. Jan, the former Miss Mississippi, was over the years the quieter of the two, rarely speaking of the family's fate or taking a stand of any kind on the events of the civil rights movement. Carla, on the other hand, remained interested in the unfolding social movements of the 1960s. After finishing her high school education in Washington DC, (the Heffners had relocated to suburban Hyattsville, Maryland), Carla studied at Sarah Lawrence College. She left not only Mississippi, but eventually the United States as well. She settled in Europe and eventually married a member of the British Parliament. According to a McComb memoirist, Carla has issued a standing invitation to her former McComb High School classmates to hold a class reunion at her and her husband's baronial ancestral home. In the spring of 1997, her father died there of cancer. Malva died, also of cancer, in 1995.[12]

Here at the fiftieth anniversary of the most important events of Mississippi's civil rights struggles, the saga of the Heffner family remains relatively unknown. No plaques, no documentaries, and very little in the historical examinations of those years marks their story. McComb itself seems never to have felt that it has anything to live down or for which to apologize, as with Oxford or Philadelphia. Other than the Heffners' obituaries, the Jackson newspaper has not seemed interested in reminding the state what happened to them in those years. Compared with other Mississippians, of course, their fate at least does not involve a cold case murder. Still, the silence over McComb and the Heffner family is striking. Surely no activist, from Bob Moses to any of the Freedom Summer volunteers, can think of the city without recalling the open campaign of bombing of 1964. The story of the Heffners was not punctuated with a murder, as in Philadelphia, or a riot, as in Oxford, but while that fact complicates its telling as a dramatic event, the story of the Heffners is too important and too revealing to be relegated to a brief sentence or two, as it merits even in histories of the civil rights movement in Mississippi. But why should the Heffners' story loom larger either in histories of the period or in the stories that McComb remembers about its history and character as a community? After all, the story of the Great Migration of African Americans from the Deep South to other parts of the United States is no better and often far worse than what happened to the Heffners, and it is no cynicism to say so. The Heffners' story matters because of the things it says about community, belonging, violence, participation, and guilt in the maintenance and unravelling of the Jim Crow order. Black McComb citizens were constantly aware of the forms of power in the city, and the consequences they were liable to face if they transgressed Jim Crow laws or community mores. The Heffners were first the beneficiaries and then the victims of that system of power and social control. It has been a hard pill for Mississippians to swallow, but it is nevertheless the truth that white Mississippians had the luxury of noticing or not noticing race as the occasion demanded. Nostalgic recollections of the old days in McComb and other southern communities can afford to forget Jim Crow because whites were allowed not to think about it. This is not precisely the same thing as saying that every white person carries guilt from those years or benefitted tangibly from the subordination of black citizens, although the latter is true. We do not make history in the ways textbooks and popular culture suggest that we can. People of McComb went about their getting and spending and lives and religious devotions asking mostly that tomorrow might be better than today and at least no worse. And considerations of responsibility are meaningless if one does not draw a distinction between those people who planted dynamite and those who wished only to live their lives without getting involved one way of another, as surely did the bulk of the white population of McComb, including my grandparents and the two high school students that summer who would become my parents in 1965. To demand that any of them should have "done something" about the conditions that prevailed that summer or in the years leading up to it is to ask more of them than most of us ask of ourselves. But southern whites (of those years and later) must understand that Jim Crow operated in McComb in a direct, visible and often violent way on the black citizens of the community, and the legacies of those years and the failure forthrightly to remember and confront them have something to do with the problems with which we contend today.

The story of the Heffners, then, shows how fragile and how strong at the same time the bonds of white community were in the Jim Crow South. And in many ways, so they remain. In what amounted to an instant, what the Heffners believed about responsibility and belonging turned on them. It is perhaps not too much to ask that in the chronicles of the Jim Crow years in Mississippi it is remembered that the Heffners suffered, too.

1. *Delta Democrat-Times*, September 9, 1964.

2. On Sweeney in the McComb period and after, see William H. Chafe, *Never Stop Running: Allard Lowenstein and the Struggle to Save American Liberalism* (New York: Basic Books, 1993), 450–59.

3. St. Louis *Post Dispatch*, September 12, 1964.

4. Hodding Carter, *So the Heffners Left McComb* (New York: Doubleday & Company, 1965).

5. For a collection of excellent recent scholarship, see Ted Ownby, ed., *The Civil Rights Movement in Mississippi* (Jackson, University Press of Mississippi, 2013). For another fine collection that assesses the influence of local studies on broader stories of the civil rights movement, see Emilye Crosby, ed., *Civil Rights History from the Ground Up: Local Struggles, A National Movement* (Athens, University of Georgia Press, 2011). The best history of the civil rights movement in Mississippi is John Dittmer, *Local People: The Struggle for Civil Rights in Mississippi* (Urbana, University of Illinois Press, 1994).

6. *New York Times*, October 6, 1911.

7. David R. Davies, "J. Oliver Emmerich and the McComb *Enterprise-Journal*: Slow Change in McComb, 1964," *Journal of Mississippi History* (57: 1 [March, 1995]), 1–23.

8. Joseph Crespino, *In Search of Another Country: Mississippi and the Conservative Counterrevolution* (Princeton: Princeton UP, 2007), 111.

9. Ann Waldron, *Hodding Carter: The Reconstruction of a Racist* (Chapel Hill, Algonquin Books, 1993).

10. Joseph Crespino, "The Strange Career of Atticus Finch," *Southern Cultures* (6: 2 [June, 2000]), 9–29.

11. Taylor Branch, *Parting the Waters: America in the King Years, 1963–1965* (New York: Simon & Schuster, 1998), 505.

12. Mac Gordon, *Hometown: A Remembrance. How a Small Town*

Newspaper and Ordinary Citizens Joined Together in the 1960s to End Racial Violence in McComb, Mississippi (Magnolia, Miss., Magnolia Gazette Publishing Company, 2011), 202–4.

SO THE HEFFNERS LEFT McCOMB

BOOKS BY HODDING CARTER II

Lower Mississippi (Rivers of America Series), 1942
Civilian Defense of the United States (with Colonel R. Ernest
  Dupuy), 1942
The Winds of Fear, 1945
Flood Crest, 1947
Southern Legacy, 1950
Gulf Coast Country (with Anthony Ragusin), 1951
*John Law Wasn't So Wrong: The Story of Louisiana's Horn of
  Plenty*, 1952
Where Main Street Meets the River, 1953
Robert E. Lee and the Road of Honor, 1954
So Great a Good (with Betty W. Carter), 1955
The Marquis de Lafayette: Bright Sword for Freedom, 1958
The Angry Scar: The Story of Reconstruction, 1959
First Person Rural, 1962
Doomed Road of Empire: The Spanish Trail of Conquest, 1963
The Ballad of Catfoot Grimes and Other Verses, 1964
So the Heffners Left McComb, 1965
The Commandos of World War II, 1966
*Their Words Were Bullets: The Southern Press in War, Recon-
  struction, and Peace* (Mercer University Lamar Memorial
  Lecture), 1969

PREFACE: The Way It Was

In the spring of 1964 the stage was set for what had been predicted would be a "long, hot summer" in the state of Mississippi. Repeated reports were made of a planned "invasion" into the state.

The United States Senate was engaged in an emotionally packed filibuster seeking to halt the passage of then-pending civil rights legislation.

National headlines and television and radio broadcasts emphasized the preparations for this invasion. There were editorials predicting a "blood bath" in Mississippi.

Photostat copies of the more severe attacks, including an editorial predicting a blood bath, were distributed in the McComb area.

The reactions of Mississippians to these threats from outside the state were expressed in resentment, frustration, and fear.

As plans were made in other areas to launch this announced invasion, there were corresponding plans made in the McComb area to resist it.

The people became inflamed. The spirit which followed was akin to patriotic fervor as men spoke of defending their families from outside attack. There developed a regional solidarity which popularized the leaders who spoke of a resistance movement.

The stage which was set for "the long, hot summer" bore evidence of becoming the scene of a reign of terror.

Both state and local governments joined in the plans of resistance. The legislature was called into special session. New laws were enacted. The strength of the state highway patrol was doubled. Auxiliary police organizations were developed at the local level. Sheriffs' offices employed added deputies.

There were no visible indications of an effort to encourage restraint. Political leadership said little about the need of exercising moderation at a time when the community powder keg was readied for an explosion.

Oliver Emmerich
Editor-Publisher
McComb *Enterprise-Journal*
December 2, 1964

SO THE HEFFNERS LEFT McCOMB

CHAPTER I

Six dozen frozen hot tamales can scarcely be thought of
as a collective instrument of personal disaster. For Albert
W. Heffner, Jr., whose friends in McComb, Mississippi,
and elsewhere call Red, and his wife, Mary Alva, better
known as Malva, they were. On the night of July 17,
1964, they served the hot tamales to the wrong people, to
wit, two young white civil rights workers, one an ordained minister.

Red and Malva purchased the tamales at Doe's in
Greenville, Mississippi, at the end of a glorious 4th of
July weekend complete with a Delta wedding and three
days of fun. On the way home they bought them there
because Doe's regionally famous tamales lean strongly to
garlic and Red and Malva like garlic.

This story is principally that of forty-two-year-old Red
and Malva who is forty but doesn't look it. They had lived
in McComb for ten years before the sharing of these
tamales made them refugees from McComb and the state
of Mississippi. It concerns, too, their seventeen-year-old
daughter Carla and Malva's nineteen-year-old daughter,

9

Jan Nave, who was Miss Mississippi for 1963–64 and whose GI father was killed in the Battle of the Bulge a month before Jan was born. The tale also has to do with the overwhelming majority of the 8000 white residents of McComb, all bound together in a unity spawned of fear. McComb is a community of 13,000 souls in Southwest Mississippi's Pike County.

There are others who can be seen against a near and far background of bombed-out and burned Negro churches and houses, the partially wrecked dwelling with the hopeful name of Freedom House, the beleaguered home in which the Heffners lived; some clergymen, mostly Episcopalian; some public officials; a newspaper editor and some newspapermen; an office-building owner; an apartment-house manager; and some young adult and student members of a group that called itself COFO, the Council of Federated Organizations, consisting mostly of college undergraduates who made an idealistic if foolhardy attempt to educate Mississippi Negroes for citizenship and to help them register in the summer of 1964, the long, hot summer. Nor can some once-friendly neighbors be overlooked. A shadowy contrapuntal chorus might be recruited from McComb's 5000 Negroes whose presence has not often been taken into serious account by the whites.

Until that summer, Red Heffner was just another youngish businessman who made a decent living, drove a 1963 Impala and a 1962 Chevy II, which were not bought for cash, and had the usual house and other notes to meet. If he was slow to pay, he was no slower than most of his contemporaries and he always paid. Because he wanted his town to prosper and grow, he took part in a variety of civic activities.

On their first day in McComb the Heffners had moved into their then uncompleted flat-top, three-bedroom home as first settlers in the rolling Carroll Oaks subdivision. They lived in the $16,000 dwelling until Labor Day weekend, 1964. By that time there were few lots remaining to be sold in Carroll Oaks. It had become the second most desirable residential area in McComb. Its homeowners were mostly junior industrial executives and younger business and professional men, some of whose homes cost as much as $40,000.

In the intervening years the Heffners had converted the carport at the front of the house into an informal den, glass-walled on two sides and with an open counter, for easy service, on the kitchen side. To keep the television set from dominating a gathering of friends, it was mounted on a shelf behind paneled doors which could be opened when there was a program those in the room wanted to see. Wall-to-wall carpeting covered the more formal living- and dining-rooms and the next project would have been a second bathroom. A tree near the front entrance, around which the house had been built, had long since died but Malva had planted a wisteria vine whose green leaves in summer and lavender blooms in the spring were supported by the dead trunk. The garden, like most of those in McComb, had its share of camellias, and Red himself had planted the camellia sasanqua hedge across the back of the property.

Red, in the last two years, had made an increasingly good living as an independent insurance agent after eight years with Blue Cross. His special field was pensions. He was proud of the three beautiful women of his household and of the recognition which he and the girls had won in the past year. Red and Malva delighted in showing visiting friends the billboards on the outskirts of their little city which proclaimed that it was the home of Jan Nave, Miss Mississippi. They liked to reminisce about their trip to Atlantic City the previous September for the Miss America contest and a holiday in Miami that spring, given as an award to Red by the Lincoln National Life Insurance Company of Fort Wayne, Indiana, for selling in excess of $2,000,000 worth of life insurance in 1963. Carla, a high school junior, who had been selected best high school actress at the Mississippi State University Drama Festival in November, had been rewarded in May with a summer scholarship to the Herbert Berghof Drama Studio in New York City. She and Jan had each been chosen in their early teens as "Future Miss Pike County." Jan's Miss Mississippi title had cost Red some $5000 in such added expenses as clothing for the womenfolk and the family's trip to Atlantic City for the Miss America Pageant. But no one minded in July 1964. The Heffners were happier and riding higher than ever before in their lives.

Two months later, none of the Heffners was a resident of McComb and only Jan, as a student at Mississippi State College for Women, remained in Mississippi.

Red Heffner had no other idea than to spend the rest of his life in McComb and the way his premium volume was rising every month he couldn't see any obstacle. He believed that he was liked, not only by the crowd at the

Country Club and the Little Theatre group but by the community at large. Six years earlier the Chamber of Commerce had given him a coveted Community Service Award for his part in McComb's effort to gain new industries. He had been president of the Pike County Little Theatre Association and state president of the Mississippi Multiple Sclerosis Association. He had helped set up the Pike County chapter of the organization working for exceptional children.

Malva had found her place, too. She had been a member of the Junior Auxiliary, a South-wide social and charitable organization modeled upon the Junior League of the larger cities, and when her five years of active service were up had become an associate. For five years she had served as president of McComb Youth Center, Incorporated, and had led the drive to raise $30,000 to build the center. In the years of fund raising she had supervised magazine sales and automobile raffles, served innumerable cookies and cokes to the young people who met in her home to organize student fund-raising projects during the building campaign, hired the director after the brick veneered concrete block building was completed, and even waxed its floors herself. Her hula at Dixie Springs Lake north of town provided the most attractive sequence in the civic movie with which McComb sought to lure new industries. She and Sid Hodges had also danced a memorable calypso at the Lions Club Annual Minstrel, and Red, who somehow has managed to keep his sense of humor, says that if they had to be run out of town, it should have been because of that performance. Like the rest of the family, Malva had acted in the Little Theatre plays and had been costume director ever since she and Red moved to McComb. She was in demand throughout the state as a beauty-pageant director and everybody gave her much of the credit when Jan was selected Miss Mississippi.

Malva and Red liked to relax with their friends, of whom they believed they had many, in the Country Club swimming pool, dining-room, and bar on Saturdays. And they usually kept their own counsel when members disclosed authoritatively that the Supreme Court and every President since Herbert Hoover were or had been Communist tools and that civil rights decisions and legislation were part of a Communist masterplot to mongrelize the race.

The more strait-laced folk of the largely Baptist town may have thought that the Heffners, along with the rest of the interwoven Country Club and Little Theatre sets, drank too much. But they were not singled out for any particular community disapproval.

They were and are extraordinarily devoted to the two girls. They cannot talk for five minutes without introducing them into the conversation.

Except for being lovely and gifted and popular, Jan and Carla are dissimilar. Jan, slim of body and of average height, is an olive-skinned brunette and much more studious than Carla. She finished McComb High School in three years. She was proficient as a swimmer and specialty dancer and paid for her own dancing lessons by assisting her teacher. She turned more to art at Mississippi State College for Women, where she stretched her Miss Mississippi and GI scholarship money by serving

14

as a student assistant to the Dean of Women. She sews beautifully and makes many of her own clothes.

It should be remembered that in July 1964 Jan had been living in a dream world for almost a year. No other girl in Mississippi enjoys the wardrobe of a Miss Mississippi or the use of a handsome automobile presented for her year as beauty queen. She had participated in Governor Paul Johnson, Jr.'s inaugural parade in Jackson and, as part of the courtesies to the governor's lady, she had presented her with a bouquet of red roses. In the spring she had represented the state of Mississippi at the inauguration of Governor John McKeithen of Louisiana, dressed in a long emerald silk satin gown with a train-type panel down the back.

In her year as Miss Mississippi Jan had gone to Atlantic City as a Miss America contestant and there danced between life-size charcoal portraits of herself which she had sketched. She had been feted in Mississippi some fifty times. It is no wonder that the harsh realities created by her parents' involvement were distasteful to her, especially since she does not have the temperament of a crusader. She was not happy over what was happening and she wanted no part of it. Neither did Harry "Brother" Wilson, member of an estimable arch-conservative planter family in the Yazoo-Mississippi Delta, the boy she would pick from a good many suitors for a husband. In his social concepts Brother was poles apart from her parents; except that Jan, like the rest of the family, had always considered segregation morally wrong, she and Brother are also poles apart from Carla in their thinking.

15

Carla, who is almost a blonde, with light, wavy hair
and gray-blue eyes, was no scholar at McComb High. Her
grades in the studies she liked were good, but she preferred to read controversial books, to write for the Mc-
Comb *Enterprise-Journal* and the McComb High School
paper, *The Tiger Rag*, and to scribble poetry that is as-
toundingly mature. She also liked the stage and acted
in the Little Theatre and school plays from the time she
was twelve.

What sets Carla further apart from her sister is her preoccupation with civil rights. The young girl had been
speaking her mind about human freedom long before she
went to school in New York. A letter she wrote from there
to her parents was as thought-revealing as any letter ever
written home by a teenager.

The Heffners had other interests besides their family
life and civic work and enjoying themselves. Among their
closer friends were the Reverend Colton Smith, vicar of
the Episcopal mission Church of the Mediator, and his
wife, Angela. The Reverend Mr. Smith is a twenty-eight-
year-old native of Vicksburg, Mississippi, who, after his
graduation from the University of the South at Sewanee,
Tennessee, took his degree in theology from the General
Theological Seminary in New York City. Angela Smith is
the British-born daughter of a former member of the staff
of the British delegation to the United Nations, and the
Smiths met in New York City. The young minister's abiding hope was to raise the mission, which could count some
150 communicants, to the status of a parish. His concern
in the summer of 1964 was to keep down racial conflict
by building understanding. It was simply because Colton

and Angela were interesting young people that Red and Malva were attracted to them.

The Heffners took their church at least as seriously as do most Episcopalians. Red, who had been a Methodist, and Malva, who had been a Baptist, had been confirmed in 1956 in McComb. Red had served on the Mission Committee, the equivalent of a parish vestry, and had become a lay reader early in 1963. When Jan, then a freshman at M.S.C.W., was selected in May of that year to represent the college in the Miss Mississippi Pageant, Red and Malva returned home early from the festivities so he could be on hand to read morning prayer at McComb and at the tiny county seat of Magnolia, seven miles to the south.

In all fairness it must be admitted that on several occasions the Heffners had not behaved in the accepted McComb tradition.

It was in 1956 that Red declined to join the formidable state-wide Citizens Council, organized in Indianola, Mississippi, a year earlier with the purpose of holding the racial line through economic, political, and social sanctions. In 1960 Red and Malva not only voted for John F. Kennedy but admitted their heresy. And in 1962 at the Ole Miss-Kentucky football game played in Memorial Stadium in Jackson, the night before the bloody Ole Miss riots, they remained in their seats in stunned horror as nearly all other Mississippians in the stadium rose to their feet and cheered in near hysteria as Governor Ross Barnett made an incendiary half-time speech. It was then that Malva wrote to the Jackson *Clarion-Ledger* a letter which that newspaper did not publish. This is the first time it has appeared in print:

17

202 Shannon Drive
McComb, Mississippi
October 3, 1962

Mr. T. M. Hederman, Editor
The Clarion-Ledger
Jackson, Mississippi

Dear Mr. Hederman:

Your paper and our governor, Ross Barnett, have done the worst possible disservice to our state of Mississippi by not guiding the people and helping them get ready for this change that is taking place in America and the South. Search your souls and ask your God if you have done the right thing by not trying to awaken your fellow Mississippians to the facts of change. We cannot separate ourselves from the past. The past cannot be carried into the future.

I quote a well-loved southern author, Lillian Smith:

"Segregation is a symbol of all we lack; a symbol of hollow men, of emptiness, a symbol of brokenness. We cannot limit this word to race relations. Our entire lives are fragmented; we are split off from the source of wholeness; we are not deeply related even to ourselves."

Some weeks ago, in our capitol city, there was an international football game. Mexican youths playing our white youths. In parts of this country, these Mexicans would not have been allowed to play with our pure white, yet in Jackson the game was widely publicized and received tremendous popular support. Take our Negroes to the same part of the country

18

that would not accept the Mexicans and they would have been accepted in the same manner that Mississippi accepted the Mexicans. Why is this?

Don't call me names. My grandfather served with the Confederate Army during the War Between the States. My first husband died in combat in the Battle of the Bulge. He and I both attended 'Ole Miss.' I feel that the American flag should fly high.

I cannot understand why so many people in my home state feel as they do. Their leadership, the politicians, clergy, and newsmen have, for a hundred years, lived in the past. They have not tried to guide people in the problems of the present. They have taken the easy way by catering to our natural pride in the achievements of our forefathers. Our forefathers were faced with problems of a hundred years ago. Our problems are with us now. If we are to survive as a great state and a great people, we must be educated to handle current problems.

We in Mississippi, along with others throughout the country, can find ourselves through love and understanding. We are created in His image—the red and yellow, the black and white.

Sincerely yours,

Malva Cooper Heffner

In November 1963 Carla burst into tears and walked out of a school student-body pep rally when Principal Percy Reeves' announcement that the President of the United States had been assassinated was greeted with the

19

kind of mass cheering usually reserved only for a winning football team. Three days later the Heffners asked that Carla be excused from school ten minutes before the noon recess to attend a memorial service for the late President at the Church of the Mediator. Although Principal Reeves had soundly reprimanded his students for their joyous approval of murder, in which they were obviously echoing their parents' sentiments, Carla was told that she must remain until the noon bell rang. Red and Malva were astounded the request was denied and Red went over the head of the principal and demanded of the superintendent of schools, Robert Simpson, that his daughter be let out. She was. Nobody else in high school was.

But on the night of July 17, most people in McComb were not much concerned with the Heffners' respect for John F. Kennedy. They had more important matters on their minds. Namely the COFO invasion and how to meet it.

The Council of Federated Organizations, COFO, was the title under which several of the principal national organizations dedicated to obtaining civil rights for Negroes joined together for work in Mississippi. Represented in COFO were the Committee on Racial Equality (CORE), the Student Nonviolent Coordinating Committee (SNCC), the National Association for the Advancement of Colored People, and the Southern Christian Leadership Conference. SNCC became the principal recruiter and director for what was termed the Mississippi Summer Project, with the National Council of Churches providing clerical advisers to the young people whose avowed primary purpose was to aid Negroes to qualify as voters.

But before the story is told of what immediately preceded and what followed the hot tamale supper, it may be helpful to know the Heffners better.

Red Heffner could be taken for an alumnus of the Baltimore Colts. A tall, burly, sandy-haired man, his light wit and large repertoire of jokes, as befits any gregarious salesman, obscure but can't hide his knowledge and enjoyment of a wide range of subjects, especially literature and psychology. His Mississippi roots do not go down as deep as do his wife's, for his farmer forebears on his father's side moved from North Carolina to Mississippi only three generations ago. In some parts of the state this Johnny-come-lately status can make a descendant still a suspect stranger. His mother was the daughter of Swedish immigrants.

Red was born in the King's Daughters Hospital in Greenwood, Mississippi. In his earlier years he lived on his father's cotton plantation near Shellmound, twelve miles north of Greenwood. He received all his secondary education in the Greenwood schools, where he was an excellent debater and played football and the clarinet in the high school band with equal mediocrity. He learned enough about farming to convince himself that he wanted no part of it.

After his graduation from Greenwood High School in 1940, he entered Tulane University in New Orleans, where he remained a year and was pledged Kappa Sigma fraternity. Now that the statute of limitations obtains, he admits that he was one of two students who stole a Freret

21

Street trolley car at Broadway and managed to get it as far as five blocks down the street to in front of the old Tulane gym where they abandoned it, all of this while its conductor and motorman were having a cup of coffee in a short-order cafe at the end of the line.

A disastrous cotton season compelled his transfer to less expensive Sunflower Junior College at Moorhead, Mississippi. At the end of that school year he found a summer job and planned to enter the University of Mississippi the coming fall. Instead, he joined the Navy, just ahead of being drafted. He was dating a secretary at the draft board and one day she phoned to say he might as well volunteer because his number was up. Assigned to the U.S.S. *Ingham*, a destroyer escort, after six weeks of boot camp and four weeks of gunnery school, he saw combat duty in the North Atlantic for sixteen months. The *Ingham's* base was Boston, but Iceland became more like home. During this time the *Ingham* was shepherding convoys on the Murmansk and other North Atlantic runs. There followed ten weeks at pharmacist's-mate school at Groton, Connecticut, and then assignment as pharmacist's mate on an Army transport, the U.S.S. *William Weigul*. The *Weigul* plied the Atlantic until V-E Day and was then ordered to the Pacific. Not until April 1946 did Red receive his honorable discharge, with the rating of pharmacist's mate first class.

That June, four years behind schedule, he enrolled in the University of Mississippi's summer school under the GI Bill. He was classified as a junior in the pre-med department in September. He had developed an interest in

22

becoming a doctor while serving in the sick bay of the *Weigul*.

Red didn't feel out of place because of his age, which was twenty-four, because at least sixty per cent of the Ole Miss male student body were also veterans of World War II. He shared with these the seriousness of purpose which few of them would have felt five years earlier.

While they were both registering for a chemistry class, he encountered Malva Nave, a girl he had known casually before the war as Malva Cooper and who had returned to the university after the death of her soldier husband. He bought her a cup of coffee after registration. On November 1, two months later, they were married, twenty months after her husband's death. Malva's nineteen-month-old baby girl, Jan, was being cared for by her parents in Forest so she could go back to school.

The young couple's first home was a single room in a private house, where they shared the bathroom with ten other roomers and furnished their own heat, a kerosene heater and cooking stove. Four months later they moved into what seemed like a sumptuous apartment of three rooms and an unshared bath in a veterans' village barracks apartment.

Their daughter Carla was born in August 1947. Red, still cherishing his idea of becoming a doctor, was permitted by the attending obstetrician to help deliver his baby.

But, in the spring, Malva and Red learned that Malva would have to undergo major and expensive surgery and Red's hope of becoming a doctor went glimmering. He would have to stop school and get a job so as to have

23

money for the operation. He left Ole Miss and went to work as a salesman for a lumber manufacturing company in Jackson, Mississippi. The Heffners rented a house there and Red studied nights until he completed the six hours he lacked for his degree. The diploma came through the mail about six months after he left school. Meanwhile, he accumulated enough money to pay for the dangerously deferred operation, which was performed in the late spring of 1949.

Many other swains besides Red would have thought Mary Alva Cooper Nave sufficient compensation for a forfeited medical career. Men had been giving Malva the second look ever since her high school days. She was a campus belle at Ole Miss before her marriage and she is a good-looking woman today, dark-haired, dark-eyed, and shapely, despite the twelve pounds she has lost since the beginning of the Heffners' time of trial.

On both sides, Malva's family goes back in Mississippi for more than a hundred years. Among her forebears have been officers of the Confederacy, members of the state legislature, the moderator of the First Baptist Convention ever held in the Territory of Mississippi. Her father, who married early and then again late, was for more than thirty years prosecuting attorney of Scott County in Central Mississippi. He also served in the state legislature, where, in the prevailing Mississippi tradition, he carried a gun. Forrest Cooper, her half-brother, thirty-two years her senior, is a conservative, respected lawyer of Indianola, Mississippi, where the Citizens Councils were born, and a one-time state commander of the American Legion and a past national vice-commander. Sidney

Cooper, her full brother, is a representative of the text-book division of an eastern publishing house. Because of the state's affinity for guilt by association and because he does business with the state, he has probably been more concerned than any other member of the family over the unfavorable attention his sister and her husband have received.

At Ole Miss, Malva was a much courted member of Kappa Delta sorority, who majored in music and excelled as a variety dancer and gymnast. With one college romance behind her, she met Bob Nave, a twenty-one-year-old Indianian who had worked briefly for the Studebaker Corporation as the youngest draftsman ever employed in the design department. A private, he had been sent to the University of Mississippi to study in the Army Student Training Program, through which the Army sought better to utilize men of superior education and ability.

But Bob's talents were not so employed. He never finished the training program, for the invasion of Europe was at hand and fresh combat manpower was needed in a hurry. He and Malva were secretly married in May 1944. Soon after, he was transferred to Camp McCain, near Grenada, Mississippi, and assigned as an infantryman in the 94th Division. When the school year ended, Malva rented a room in Grenada, where Bob joined her on weekend passes. He went overseas in late summer and Malva returned to her parents in Forest.

Malva never saw Bob again. In February 1945 she received formal War Department notification that he was missing in action. On March 19 Jan was born, four days

25

before Malva turned twenty-one. That fall the War Department confirmed Bob's death. Malva wasn't sure of what she wanted to do with her life, but in September of 1946 she re-entered the university as a junior.

As with thousands of other veterans, Red made a couple of false starts before he found a job that suited him. He stayed with the lumber company for more than two years, during the last ten months of which he and Malva lived outside the state of Mississippi, in Trenton, Tennessee, for the first and only time in their lives. Here four-year-old Jan was stricken with a happily light case of polio and, to strengthen a slightly weakened leg, Malva entered her in a dancing school.

When the Korean War began, Red remembered that a kinsman had made a small fortune during World War II in the tire-recapping business. The Heffners had been able to put aside a little money and Red used his $4500 savings and another $4500 which he borrowed to buy a half interest in a recapping firm in Greenville, Mississippi, fifty miles west of his home town. With 40,000 population, it was the largest city in the Yazoo-Mississippi Delta.

The enterprise went on the rocks when a fire destroyed building, equipment, and supplies. The insurance paid only the company's creditors and the $4500 of borrowed capital.

During the three years the family lived in Greenville, Red was active in the Kiwanis Club, the Junior Chamber of Commerce, Trinity Methodist Church, and in politics as the campaign manager for Joseph Wroten, a young lawyer, in his successful first quest for a seat in the state House of Representatives. What is significant here is that Joe Wroten was to be one of the two truly liberal members of the Mississippi legislature during the twelve years he served. The Heffners made lasting friends in Greenville, but some of Malva's fellow Baptists criticized her for teaching in the Catholic parochial school.

After the recapping business failed, the Heffners went to Forest and took a small apartment. In a short while Red learned from a private employment service in Jackson that the Blue Cross, a relatively young organization in Mississippi, the last state to endorse the program, had an opening for a field representative in its non-group department. He got the job, which entailed traveling all over the state out of the Jackson office. He was promoted to the group department in four months and was transferred to McComb as district group representative.

The Heffners moved into the unfinished house at 202 Shannon Drive in Carroll Oaks June 23, 1954, their first day in McComb. Neither lights nor water, gas nor telephone had been connected, but their furniture was on its way.

For the next eight years Red traveled through the nine Southwest Mississippi counties which made up his district, servicing established groups, organizing new ones, and upgrading existing employer-employee groups as the cost of medical care increased. His work brought him a succession of raises until his earnings at the time he went into business for himself came to around $9000 a year. During the eight years he was never lower than

27

fourth in performance ranking among the Blue Cross representatives in the state.

But Red was dissatisfied with the income limitations in the Blue Cross organization and disturbed over a personality conflict with one of the Blue Cross executives. All this time he had been selling in competition with private group insurance companies and a friend in one such company had been urging him for four years to become an independent agent himself. Red put off making such a break because the failure of the Greenville venture had made him more than ordinarily security conscious. But when he finally made up his mind to strike out on his own, he talked to representatives of several of the major insurance companies. The best prospects for the future seemed to lie with the Lincoln National, one of the nation's top ten, so Red joined the company as an agent in September 1962. Red continued to use his home as an office, despite Malva's long-time irritation over it, until February 1964 when, because of the steady growth of his business, he was able to rent an office in the newly completed J. E. Alford Building, the most modern and advantageously situated in town. Red moved his office furniture from home and a sign went up: Albert W. Heffner, Jr., Life Insurance—Pensions—Group. Red knew that he had arrived.

Less than six months later he was given eleven days to move out.

CHAPTER II

The guests who ate the thawed-out hot tamales that Friday night in July had not been expected for supper. Red and Malva had met one of them, the Reverend Don McCord, a twenty-five-year-old minister of the Disciples of Christ, at the vicarage of the Church of the Mediator four nights before. McCord had come to McComb as a representative of the National Council of Churches to help provide guidance for some of the 700 COFO summer project workers in the state. The other, whom Red had never seen before, was clean-cut Dennis Sweeney of Portland, Oregon, a twenty-one-year-old senior and history major at Stanford University, who was a staff member of the Student Nonviolent Coordinating Committee. Red might have recognized him from the picture which had appeared in the McComb *Enterprise-Journal*, showing the handsome young blond standing in front of the bombed Negro home which served as local COFO headquarters. Before they were introduced to the neat, bespectacled young minister at the vicarage, the Heffners had never met a civil rights worker.

29

That same Monday—and Red noted the coincidence in his diary—he had driven by the bombed house on Wall Street after dropping Essie Martin, their maid. It was not the first Negro structure to have been burned or bombed since the beginning of the summer. But this was the first that Red had seen.

Red and Malva met Don McCord because the Reverend Colton Smith set up an after-supper coffee at the vicarage so that a few McComb and Magnolia people who could still listen would learn from McCord what COFO's objectives were and the part that the National Council of Churches would play in the program. Besides the Smiths and the Heffners, those who came to the vicarage that Monday night were Ragland Watkins, III, a local architect and, like Red, a lay reader; the Reverend Eldon Weisheit, the McComb Lutheran minister, and a visiting friend of his from Natchez; Aubrey Jerome Ford of Magnolia, whom everyone calls Jonah, a twenty-nine-year-old instructor in German at the University of Mississippi; white-haired Mrs. James Price, born and reared in Virginia, the widow of a prominent Magnolia attorney and a recent appointee to the Advisory Committee for Mississippi to the Civil Rights Commission; and the man they had been invited to meet, the Reverend Mr. McCord. They learned that evening that the young minister was a Yale Divinity School graduate who had spent about three years in Germany as a student and part-time teacher at the John F. Kennedy School for German and American children in Berlin. Jonah, who had been visiting at Yale with a German professor, had met the young minister at the time of his graduation. McCord talked freely and movingly of what COFO hoped to accomplish in and for Mississippi, and the Pike countians were impressed and also relieved by what he told them. COFO's interest, he said, was voter registration, and no demonstrations for integration of public facilities were planned for the summer.

Not until the bombings and the church burnings began did Red concern himself actively with the deteriorating relationship between whites and Negroes, although he had talked about the developing crisis with Colton Smith and a few selected friends. By July 1, three homes of Negroes identified with the civil rights movement had been bombed, the son-in-law of a Negro minister had been beaten, and white citizens were organizing a protection association. On the way back from the Delta, Red decided that he personally had to do something to help avoid a complete collapse of communication between the races. So two days after he and Malva got home he telephoned two Negroes whom he knew well and respected. One was Allen Coney, a Pike County school principal, with whom he had worked every fall in connection with the teachers' Blue Cross group insurance program and for whose afflicted child Red was trying to gain admission into a treatment center. The other was Earl Moses, a shoe repairman, who for years had put the taps on the girls' dancing shoes. Red asked each of them to let him know what was going on in the Negro areas and to call on him for help if they needed it. He also warned Moses that, because of the similarity of names, he was being mistaken for Robert Moses, a widely known Negro civil rights organizer whose activities had antagonized most white Mississippians. The family should move to the rear of their home, Red told Moses, as they would be safer there if someone tossed a bomb.

He also wrote two letters that day. One was to Erle Johnston, Jr., no racist bigot but the director of the Mississippi Sovereignty Commission, which is dedicated to defending and preserving the "Mississippi way of life." Red had known Johnston, the publisher of the weekly Scott County *Times* in Forest, Malva's home town, for years. The other was to Alfred P. "Bo" Statham, administrative assistant to U. S. Senator John Stennis of Mississippi and formerly a Carroll Oaks neighbor.

To each he told of his worry over the tinder-box situation in Mississippi and asked that by virtue of their positions Johnston urge the governor and "Bo" use his influence with the senator to get them to advise the people of Mississippi to stand for law and order, no matter how repugnant to them were the activities of COFO and the Civil Rights Act which President Lyndon Johnson had signed July 2.

For a man who had hitherto not involved himself in controversial issues, Red Heffner was moving in fast.

An innocuously stated request was subsequently issued by Senator Stennis on July 17, which ironically happened to be the night of the tamales. But life continued pretty much as usual for the Heffners. Thursday, Lorna and Atkins Williams, whose son had been the groom at the wedding and who runs a supermarket on the edge of Burgland, the Negro part of town; Harry Raddon, manager of the Holiday Inn Motel; Ben Lasseter, a friend

32

from Birmingham; and Mrs. Philip Enochs helped Malva and Red fry fish on their patio.

At 3:55 in the morning Moses telephoned Red. The COFO headquarters had been bombed. Red knew now that much more would have to be done in McComb than any responsible persons were doing.

That was why he welcomed the invitation to meet the COFO adviser when Colton Smith extended it.

After the meeting, Red and Malva, who liked to have people in their home and were almost always the first to invite a newcomer, brought Don McCord out to their house. They especially wanted to talk to him about student exchange programs because they thought Jan might want to go abroad for further study after she graduated.

In the morning a good Mississippi friend in government in Washington phoned unexpectedly. He was in a position to know and had heard authoritatively that there was a strong possibility that Pike County would be placed under martial law if the violence continued. Red reacted typically. During the day he went to Mayor Gordon Burt's office to tell him and found him in a hurry to get to a scheduled city board meeting. Warren Wild, then executive vice-president of the Mechanics State Bank, had listened more attentively. Red told him he didn't want to get too deeply involved because it could kill his business. Wild replied that if there were soldiers on every corner his business would be dead anyway.

Red felt the least he could do was to speak with the Reverend Wyatt Hunter, minister of McComb's First Baptist Church, and the Reverend Gault Robertson, minister of the J. J. White Presbyterian Church, about the

33

possibility of McCord's addressing their men's clubs. The Presbyterian Church is a member organization of the National Council of Churches and so, Red thought, the Presbyterians might have added reason to hear one of the Council's representatives. And the Baptists, who formed a majority of the fear-plagued community, might become less apprehensive after learning of COFO's goals. But both ministers said that an invitation to the National Council minister to address their men's clubs was completely out of the question. "The subject is entirely too volatile," one said.

That Tuesday evening Don McCord telephoned Red to say that the Reverend H. Hansel Stembridge, a Southern Baptist minister presently living in Westlake, California, and his daughter, Janie, were in Mississippi to visit the various COFO headquarters and were now in McComb. He asked that he be allowed to bring them and Mendy Samstein, a staff member of SNCC, to the Heffners' home. The Baptist minister was also visiting former fellow seminarians of the Louisville, Kentucky, Baptist Seminary to try to persuade them to take a stand against the violence which had greeted the COFO intruders in Mississippi. Red answered that they would be welcome. He knew that many of his fellow citizens would have disapproved of his hospitality, but he saw in the forthcoming visit another opportunity to learn what these people were doing in Mississippi. During the evening he pointed out to them ways that the COFO workers were needlessly antagonizing the community or could do so. He told them they ought to discourage the beatnik look affected by some of the young workers. He stressed that

34

the white boys and Negro girls should never go grocery shopping together so as to avoid the implication that they were living together. And he got Don to agree that the girl workers would be moved out of the Freedom House at once.

The evening's conversation brought out that Mr. Stembridge was a former classmate of Malva's first cousin, who is now president of the Baptist Seminary at Buenos Aires, Argentina. Since Southerners delight especially in seeking out even the remotest ties of kinship or interlocking friendship, this connection made the visitors seem that much more a part of the mainstream of the Heffners' lives.

But the most important matter discussed was the meeting between members of the COFO group and Sheriff R. R. Warren of Pike County, which had been arranged by Oliver Emmerich, editor-publisher of the McComb *Enterprise-Journal*, for the following day at the sheriff's office at the courthouse in Magnolia. Red, who had been in daily contact with his friend Oliver, knew the plans for the as yet unpublicized meeting.

McCord had visited the newspaper office a number of times and the editor kept suggesting to him that it might be possible to accomplish voter registration without turmoil if COFO would be willing to try first to "do it the easy way," as the editor put it. The sheriff had told Emmerich in May that he would not oppose orderly Negro registration. Because of this, Emmerich believed that if the workers visited Sheriff Warren and told him what they planned to do and what they did not plan to do, it might turn out that the area of agreement was larger than either side believed.

When McCord agreed to the meeting, the minister's first idea was to take a racially mixed group to the interview. Emmerich argued that, in line with his plea to "do it the easy way," only whites should attend the first meeting. His theory was that once this was successfully held, subsequent conferences might be integrated.

This was the way plans for the meeting stood Tuesday night.

But Malva and Red, who now knew how tactful Don could be, urged that it would be even better if he went alone as representative of COFO.

At first Don demurred. Three young COFO workers had been missing since June 22. They had last been seen in Neshoba County. Their bodies were later found eighteen feet under an earthen farm dam near Philadelphia, Mississippi. Because of the racial turmoil in the state, the members of COFO had made it a rule never to travel alone. To get around this argument, Red promised to spend the afternoon working in Magnolia and to follow Don back to McComb. He gave him the telephone number where he could be reached after the conference.

Later in the evening Malva said that she and Red had received from their daughter Carla a letter of which they were proud and that she would like to read it to the group. It had come just before they left for the Delta wedding. It seemed incredible to them, she said, that their child, off in New York away from them, would be going through the same self-examination that they were. She read the letter aloud:

36

"June 29, 1964

"To my dear parents,

"Growing up is not a simple task. It involves so much that adults forget during the span that separates them from our world. I have always felt fortunate to have parents who were always willing to allow me the privilege of adulthood if I could act accordingly. It is because of this closeness I feel toward my parents, and also the fact that I love them, that I am writing this letter. For the first time in my life I have truly begun to think, and although my parents may disagree with many of my thoughts, I feel they deserve to know of them. Because of the liberal attitude towards my reading, writing and listening, it is somewhat the Heffners' fault that I have had this sudden stimulation of thought. . . . I have had the background which calls for thought . . . but only now have I faced the challenge of true thinking, and through this, I find mere thinking inadequate.

"I have not been totally blind for seventeen years. I have seen much to remember as beautiful and I have seen much to cringe at in horror. Yet, there is so very much I have never seen. I have never seen these things because they did not affect me, in my sheltered pretty way of life. Nothing has been hidden, and yet, it has not been in clear view.

"Last night I attended a SNCC rally for civil rights workers journeying to my state, Mississippi, today and tomorrow. As I sat listening to Mr. Foreman, students from Mississippi and others, telling these people, 1500 in number, about a vicious, almost re-

37

tarded in their thinking, group of people who are called Mississippians, I wanted so miserably to stand up and yell, 'No! No! You're wrong!' But how could I do this? Mother . . . Daddy . . . They are right.

"I sat there as they told of life in Greenwood, where I was born . . . and as they told of life in McComb, where I live. I wonder how the Camellia City of America would feel knowing their public image is one of the most horrifying imaginable.

"And then I talked to kids who weren't much older than I. They were older though, and they were more frightened, and much braver than I have ever been. Here they were . . . with a belief so strong, they were going 1500 miles for it. It's so sad. I haven't been 15 minutes from it and I could not do anything. But these kids were risking more than even I had to lose.

"'It's a privilege to live in McComb.' Is it such a damn privilege to die there?

"I wish there was something I could do. I want to do what I feel is my obligation as an American, and I hope that doesn't sound trite—but I want to do what I feel is my responsibility as the Mississippian I am. It is a shame, truly, that I should be torn between these two. I hope I haven't upset you two who are closest to me with all of these confused thoughts and emotions, but it has become almost an obsession. It is very hard to sit still.

"I realize that in a very short time I will be returning to McComb and must again become a quiet spectator in this most gruesome game. But I am asking you to try to understand some of what I feel and am putting so poorly, and I am asking you to trust me this summer—to do what I can do, to realize what I can't do.

"Please don't dismiss this as a letter of impetuous youth.

"I guess that is all I can say, all I can ask.

I love you very much,

Carla

"P.S. Don't let my epistle on the evils of America alarm you . . . I mean I'm really not an extremist or racist or crusader.

"I must go to class now (with my Negro teacher!).

Much love,

Carla"

Mendy Samstein, who had been a close friend of Michael Schwerner, one of the missing COFO workers, had tears in his eyes before Malva finished reading the letter.

By coincidence, Carla, a few minutes later, made one of her customary after 9 P.M. collect phone calls. And her parents introduced her to Don by telephone.

McCord's meeting with the sheriff on Wednesday was both amicable and apparently fruitful. Oliver Emmerich left shortly after introducing them. Don told the sheriff just what he had told the gathering at the Smiths' the previous Monday, and Sheriff Warren promised fair treatment and no harassment as long as the COFO workers behaved in the manner which Don promised him they would.

Red, as agreed, followed Don to the Heffner home.

They arrived there around five o'clock without incident. The Emmerichs came by before supper but didn't stay long.

Early that evening the Reverend Colton Smith, Mrs. James Price, and Jonah Ford joined McCord at the Heffners' to hear what had happened at the sheriff's office. After they had eaten some of Malva's spaghetti, Red tried to reach Chief of Police George Guy, a conscientious and competent police officer who directed McComb's eighteen-man force and whose office is elective. Red wanted to tell him of the successful conference in Magnolia and suggest a similar one for the chief and the mayor, but Guy was out. The Heffners made two other telephone calls. One was to their long-time friend, Professor James M. Silver of the University of Mississippi. They had just read his *Mississippi: The Closed Society* and had sent him a copy of Carla's letter. They knew he would be interested in the opening of the channel of communication between McCord and the sheriff. While little was accomplished, the mere fact of the meeting seemed so hopeful Silver expressed the wish that he, for instance, might also be able to talk with Erle Johnston. Malva agreed to try to arrange a luncheon date for the two and called Johnston then and there. But Johnston said that such a meeting would be possible only if the professor, currently because of his book the most unpopular man in the state, would first tender his resignation from his state-paid position.

Thursday morning Red talked to Chief Guy about the Magnolia meeting the day before and told him that Oliver would have a story about it in the *Enterprise-*

Journal that afternoon. The chief thanked him, saying that until then he had been unaware that such a meeting had taken place. Red hoped that the chief and Mayor Gordon Burt would have a similar meeting after the story appeared, but he didn't suggest it.

Red spent that day at the office, working out pension programs for a beer distributor, a wholesale grocery company, and a theatre chain.

His routine was briefly broken just before he left for home by two FBI agents who dropped in to ask some questions about an incident which occurred over the weekend and which indirectly involved Jan. She had told her parents and Colton Smith of the matter. While she was home for the weekend between appearances as Miss Mississippi, she and Marty Bee, her house guest, and a casual date had attended a Saturday-night movie. After the show the boy suggested that they go by Pete's Drive-In and pick up some beer to take to the Heffners'. While they were waiting for the carhop to bring out the beer, three or four white youths, including some of Jan's former schoolmates, drove alongside and bragged to the trio about having just raised hell on Summit Street in a Negro section of town. They held up chains and pipes. A day or so afterward they were arrested on charges of shooting at McComb's first, and recently appointed, Negro policeman. The defendants were later convicted of disturbing the peace but, for insufficient evidence, the shooting charge was dismissed. The FBI agents had learned through Colton Smith that Jan had seen the boys at Pete's Drive-In. They told Red they wanted to question her. Red repeated what she had told him and said

41

she would not be able to see the agents until next week, as she had gone out of town for two more appearances and would spend the weekend with her grandmother in Forest.

When Red got home that evening, in high spirits because he believed he might get all three pension accounts he had been working on, Malva wasn't as excited over his optimistic news as he had expected her to be. Only a few minutes earlier she had received the Heffners' first anonymous telephone call, albeit a friendly one. The speaker said he understood the Heffners had had civil rights workers in their home and recommended in a kindly way that the mistake not be repeated.

"My reaction was to get mad as hell," Red says. "To my knowledge no one had made a payment on that house but me and I thought I could have anyone there I damn well pleased without being bothered. We found out different."

Oliver Emmerich's front-page editorial in the *Enterprise-Journal* about the meeting in Magnolia was a forthright, potentially helpful one. The editorial read:

SHERIFF CONFERS WITH CR WORKER

An Editorial

By Oliver Emmerich

In this day of uncertainties and doubts, of fears and apprehension, it is helpful to report on developments which lessen fears and frustrations—and which contribute to the cause of tranquility.

We believe this report on a conference between

Sheriff R. R. Warren and one of the civil rights workers in McComb will help to lessen tensions in our area.

The conference was held Wednesday afternoon in the office of Sheriff Warren in the courthouse in Magnolia. The conference was between the Pike County sheriff and the Rev. Don McCord, a graduate of the School of Divinity of Yale University and a Christian minister from the State of Kansas.

When the conference opened Sheriff Warren said, "First I would like to know your objectives. What are the purposes of the civil rights workers in McComb?"

The minister replied, "First, I would like to tell you what we do not plan to do.

"First, we do not plan to attempt any cafe or theatre sit-ins.

"Second, we do not plan to worship in your churches contrary to your customs.

"Third, we plan no demonstrations of any kind."

The sheriff greeted this pronouncement with obvious satisfaction. He asked, "And what do you plan to do?"

Replied the minister, "Our program will be purely educational. This is a major staff decision. Any civil rights worker who does not want to restrict his work to this field in McComb or Mississippi is invited to leave."

The sheriff agreed that local people are not opposed to educational programs.

Said the civil rights leader, "We want to work in the area of orderly voter registration and voter qualifications. We are trying to stimulate the desire to learn. We are trying to discourage school drop-outs.

43

We will have a recreational program for young people."

Sheriff Warren assured the civil rights worker of full protection of the law. He said, "If you have individuals who want to take the voter registration test you will have the full cooperation of my office." He added, "All I ask is that you folks conduct yourselves in an orderly manner." The minister responded that this was his purpose.

Sheriff Warren added that he was fully confident that Circuit Clerk Glen Fortenberry would apply all voter tests fairly, regardless of race.

The conference between Sheriff Warren and the Rev. Mr. McCord was marked by courtesy and understanding. There were no unpleasantries.

Said the Rev. Mr. McCord, "The term 'freedom school' has conjured up many false ideas. I assure you that our work will be exclusively in the field of education."

Replied Sheriff Warren, "Our people are not opposed to education. We are trying to educate all of our people, white and colored alike."

The Rev. Mr. McCord said that he had seen the new school in Burgland and that he was impressed by it.

It was quite obvious to anyone listening in on the conference that both Sheriff Warren and the minister were speaking with good faith and honest intentions.

In agreeing to the interview Sheriff Warren made a statesmanlike effort and rendered a helpful service to all of our people.

This conference was a helpful civic service in that it invalidated many disturbing rumors and has

44

brought into the open the announced program of the civil rights workers—"no cafe or theatre sit-ins, no church worship contrary to custom, no demonstrations"—"an educational program exclusively."

Sheriff Warren, in establishing definitely what is planned and the procedures involved, has furthered the best interests of all of our people.

After the paper appeared, Red tried to reach Sheriff Warren to compliment him on the meeting and to tell him that he and Oliver would try to arrange a similar conference between the mayor, the chief of police, and McCord, an incidental purpose being to take part of the political pressure off the sheriff for conferring with the outsider. Unfortunately, Sheriff Warren was away from home, so Red only exchanged pleasantries with Mrs. Warren.

The next morning, Friday, July 17, Malva invited Colton and Angela Smith to come after evening prayer and share the six dozen frozen hot tamales. But either Malva had not been specific about time and occasion or Angela misunderstood her invitation. The result was that when Malva phoned that night to ask why the Smiths were so late, Angela had already started preparing supper.

An incontrovertible fact about frozen hot tamales that have been thawed and heated is that they have to be eaten soon or thrown away. And there they were, six dozen of them and just Red and Malva to undertake to consume them. It was natural for Red to think of inviting the personable young minister, who was expected later anyhow for a meeting with the Smiths and themselves,

45

to help eat the hot tamales, which would otherwise go to waste. So the Heffners asked Don to come early and he accepted. Don asked if he could bring someone else and Red agreed instinctively. The someone was Dennis Sweeney, the SNCC staff worker from Stanford. They came right over and the four of them sat down before the big platter of tamales.

Only seconds after the last tamales had been eaten and just as the Smiths were coming in the front door, Carla telephoned again from New York to tell her parents of her latest adventures in the big city.

In the course of the conversation Malva told Carla that Don—whom she had met by telephone three nights earlier —and a friend, named Dennis Sweeney, were there and had been sharing in Doe's hot tamales. Later in the conversation, Carla repeated the name Dennis Sweeney, asking if she hadn't seen his picture in the *Enterprise-Journal*.

So it was that Dennis' full name was spoken twice. In the light of immediately subsequent events, it would appear probable that someone else was listening in.

After Malva had cleared the table, everyone settled down in the den to discuss the hoped-for meeting between the mayor, the chief of police, and Don. It is extraordinary that to this day Red and Malva can't figure out why they were concerning themselves so greatly with trying to create an element of understanding in their tense little city.

"It was more than one thing," Red said months later when McComb was only a part of their past. "The disappearance of those boys in Philadelphia was the shocker. I didn't want to have any more kids killed in Mississippi.

46

But there was more to it than that. Carla's letter from New York was part of it. So was the meeting at the vicarage. Probably most of all it was how reasonable everything Don McCord said seemed to be. And don't forget I was worried about the image of my town. You don't get new industries by burning houses of God and beating up people. It just seemed the right thing to do at the time."

About ten minutes later the telephone rang again. Malva answered. A woman's voice asked: "Can I speak to Dennis Sweeney?"

Assuming the caller was someone from COFO headquarters, Malva handed Dennis the receiver.

As Dennis related it afterward, the voice asked him how the civil rights work was coming along. He answered: "Pretty well, I guess," trying to think who the caller might be. The voice then asked if he were a friend of the Heffners. Having met them for the first time only a short hour or so before and having partaken of their favorite dish, which, not being a garlic lover, he had not particularly liked, he answered tentatively, "Yes, I guess so." But by now a wary combat veteran after several weeks in McComb, he recognized the danger in continuing the conversation and explained to his caller that he didn't want to talk further until the speaker identified herself. The anonymous caller hung up.

Dennis rejoined the group and everyone talked about the mysterious queries and wondered how his presence at the Heffners' was known. Don said no one at headquarters would have told an outsider where Dennis was because no worker ever disclosed the whereabouts of an-

47

other unless he was satisfied of the good intent of the inquirer.

Although they did not know it at first, automobiles were already beginning to encircle the house, which stood on a corner atop a small rise. Because of the corner's steep incline and sharp turn, any automobile ascending the street automatically shifts into second gear. Soon the collective lower notes became audible to those in the house, even over the hum of the air-conditioner. Red's curiosity was only casual at first, but the others were almost immediately disturbed by the sudden build-up of traffic in a residential area. However, no one looked out and the conversation went on.

Some ten minutes later the telephone rang again. This time the speaker identified himself as D. B. Dekle, a resident of Carroll Oaks and a business acquaintance of Red's, who was manager of a McComb funeral home and a one-time insurance agent. The two men occasionally talked shop, but neither had ever been in the other's home. Dekle asked Red: "Whose car is that in front of your house?"

"My first thought was to tell him it's none of your business, D.B.," Red says. "But I knew how upset our town already was and I didn't want to make things any worse. So I very carefully explained who was there, made reference to the editorial about the meeting the day before, and told him we were now discussing the possibility of a similar meeting with city officials. Dekle seemed satisfied with the explanation. All he said was O.K."

Obviously nervous now because of the second phone call, Don and Dennis decided to leave. Before going,

Don telephoned the FBI headquarters in the Holiday Inn Motel and for their information told them of the strange sequence of telephone calls. He said that someone must have monitored the Heffners' phone to discover Dennis' presence. He then gave Red the FBI telephone number in case he should want it. Colton offered to follow the COFO car out of the neighborhood.

Red opened the front door. Now those inside discovered why the sound of motors had increased. Ringing the corner, with their headlights trained on the house, eight to ten automobiles were parked, their engines running. Red told himself that after the people in the waiting automobiles saw him they would realize there was no need for the demonstration. Practically blinded by the headlights, he led the way down the front walk. The COFO workers' car was partially blocked by one of the cars surrounding the house, but the Smiths' was not. Colton and Angela got in their automobile, which was parked behind Dennis', and Colton backed up a few feet to give Dennis room to turn around in the driveway, as the Heffners watched in the glare of the headlights. Colton U-turned in the street so as to be immediately behind Don and Dennis and the four drove away from Carroll Oaks. The waiting automobiles fell in behind them.

After the Philadelphia disappearances, most COFO cars in Mississippi had been equipped with two-way radios. So were the various COFO headquarters to which they were attached. By radio, Don and Dennis now arranged that they should be met at the Church of the Mediator by an escort from their headquarters. By the time the pair reached the church, two carloads of workers had already

49

arrived. They were able to get the license numbers of some of the trailing automobiles from Carroll Oaks to turn over to the FBI. Back in the house, Red telephoned the FBI and reported the incident. The agent who answered told him it was a matter for the local police, which it was, as the FBI has no authority to intervene in local police matters. When Red telephoned police headquarters, the desk sergeant who answered said he would send someone to check on the safety of the COFO workers and that the police would come by his house.

No policeman turned up at the Heffner home. So after waiting half an hour Red got out his shotgun and loaded his .38 automatic and put it in a trousers pocket. The pistol, rarely handled, was in one drawer and, as a safety measure, the clip was in another. But which drawer neither Malva nor Red could remember. It took some while to find the two parts and put them together. Then the tense couple crossed the street to the home of their long-time neighbors and good friends, Peter and Helen Hallin.

Pete Hallin, formerly of Jamestown, New York, is executive vice-president of Croft Metal Products, fabricators of aluminum windows and doors, and a man who, because of the firm's economic importance to McComb, is reasonably safe from community pressures. The Hallins offered the Heffners a drink and over it they discussed the disturbing events of the night. Before the Heffners left the Hallins', another friend and neighbor, Norwood Prestridge, dropped in. The next day he told Helen Hallin that as he walked across her yard to his own home next door a policeman had drawn up in a patrol car and commented to him that the folks in Carroll Oaks were sure out to get the Heffners. But no policeman came to the Heffners' home.

Meanwhile, a troubled Chief Guy had driven to COFO headquarters in his pajamas, robe, and bedroom slippers to ask if anyone wanted to prefer any charges. There was nothing to charge anyone with.

The Heffners turned out their lights and watched automobiles returning to the homes in their neighborhood. Red tried to telephone D. B. Dekle, but his phone didn't answer.

This is how it started. The start was also the beginning of the finish for the Heffners. But they didn't know it then.

CHAPTER III

According to local legend there would be no McComb, Mississippi, today had not a puritanical Yankee become concerned in 1872 over the impact of sinful New Orleans upon the morals of the employees of the railroad of which he was president.

Colonel Henry Simpson McComb's moral scruples may or may not have been a factor in his moving the shop, roundhouse, and anything else that could be transported, including the employees, away from New Orleans. The line was moving northward and he needed a terminal farther up the track. The site he chose, 105 miles up from New Orleans, was in a lovely rolling land of virgin pine and blackjack oak and occasional farms cleared from the forest by the forebears of those who tilled them. The location which Colonel McComb of Wilmington, Delaware, selected proved to be an excellent one. Streets were laid out and lots offered for sale to employees at a reasonable price so as to encourage home ownership. In a few years the village, whose official name is still McComb City, began developing into what it has remained, the most populous and industrialized town on the Illinois Central between New Orleans and Jackson, Mississippi. Three miles to the north is Summit and seven miles to the south is Magnolia, the seat of Pike County, each having grown up around stations arbitrarily established by the railroad before the Civil War at ten-mile intervals along its track. Neither of these small towns has grown appreciably in the past fifty years and most of their residents live in a past that antedates a half-century span, as even the most casual perusal of the local weeklies attests.

McComb is still a railroad town and Pike County is sawmill country and dairy country. By no stretch of the imagination can it be thought of as plantation country either in the average acreage of its farms or in the cultural background of its landowners. Few of the ancestors of Pike County farmers ever reached the affluence of slave ownership. There is no tradition in the area of that patriarchal regard for one-time black chattels, which can still be found, though decreasingly, on the plantations along the Mississippi River. Following the advice in the 1930s of a native son, two-term Governor Hugh White of Mississippi, the city and county early were successful in attracting industries. More latterly oil has been found within a whoop and a holler of the town, a discovery which provided a temporary economic boost to McComb. The Little Creek Field was opened in 1958 and a year later the discovery well of the McComb Field, some of which is within the city limits, was brought in.

Years ago an old Negro woman known only as Aunt Caroline tended her few camellia plants so lovingly and with such a green thumb that she was able to give cuttings

53

to her many friends, both white and Negro. Through the years the little switches have grown into mammoth bushes, some reaching to second-story windows. The town glories in these. When the magnificent Bellingrath Gardens were being landscaped in Alabama, many of the largest plants were purchased here and removed to the Bellingrath place. Nevertheless, enough remained and enough new ones have been grown to permit the town to use as its motto "The Camellia City of America." McComb holds an annual camellia show in which fanciers from all over the Deep South exhibit, and the town itself in winter is brilliant with rich red, delicate pink, creamy white, and multi-hued camellia bushes. Even the most ramshackle Negro cabin is almost certain to have its camellias in the front yard.

During the 1920s the flower-loving citizens also began planting azaleas, now of luxuriant size. In 1949 a Methodist minister who had been a missionary in Korea proposed, through the *Enterprise-Journal*, that the town should light its azaleas when they were at the peak of their bloom, as was customary in Japan during the cherry-blossom season. Ever since then a lighted azalea trail draws visitors from a hundred and more miles away each spring, and an azalea king and queen are crowned as part of the parade and ball which has helped to project for McComb an image of a people devoted to horticulture and beauty.

But, sorrowfully, McComb's more recent recognition must come from its undisputed eminence as the church-bombing capital of the nation. Of the more than fifty bombings or burnings of Negro churches which took place in Mississippi in 1964, McComb or Pike County night riders very capably handled the matches or Molotov cocktails or dynamite in two-thirds of such demonstrations. The community also deserves at least dishonorable mention for last year's crop of beatings of Negro and white civil rights workers.

Nor have visiting or even home-town journalists been overlooked. A Yankee correspondent for *Life* magazine was knocked through a plate-glass window by a loyal Southerner who was arrested and received the usual wrist-slap fine for this locally popular form of breach of peace. Boys will be boys, and the physical presence of a reporter from *Life* was adequate provocation in Mississippi.

McComb is pleasant to the eye. There are few homes which proclaim affluence but there are many which indicate that their owners are well-to-do or in comfortable circumstances and love the ground on which they dwell. In relation to its total population, McComb has gone in for more federally financed public housing and slum clearance on a segregated basis than any other town in Mississippi except Tupelo. And, except in two blighted areas, the city has a clean look not ordinarily associated with the bi-racial towns of the Deep South.

Although no new industries of consequence have been established in McComb in the past ten years, the city is far more industrialized than most of the other principal Mississippi communities. Spokesmen for the Southwest Mississippi Industrial Development Corporation, a regional tax-supported body whose sole purpose is to attract plants to the region, privately admit what is publicly denied, namely that a paramount reason for the recent lag is the racially motivated violence which has cursed city and county since the Supreme Court's public school decision in 1954 and especially in the last three years.

The fifteen sizable industries in McComb and Pike County employ some 5000 workers, about equally divided between residents of McComb and the surrounding countryside. They turn out such items as ladies' lingerie—because of which McComb also claims the distinction of being "The Panty Capital of the Nation"—wire-bound boxes, paper boxes, creosoted building products, aluminum windows and doors, livestock feed, and woven bedspreads. Although the Illinois Central roundhouse was abandoned and torn down after the line's conversion to Diesel-powered locomotives, the railroad still has some 800 men on its payroll here, McComb's largest.

A majority of these industrial employees, as well as a majority of McComb's other citizens, come from pioneer yeoman farmer or railroading families. The background of the Negro minority is multi-tribal slavery. Because New Orleans is less than three hours away, the more well-to-do citizens have a sophistication not always found in towns of comparable population elsewhere in the Mississippi interior.

Outwardly its business area duplicates that of a thousand other small American cities. The Chamber of Commerce lists two banks, four movies, fifteen chain stores, twenty-nine churches, two private hospitals. The hospitals have a combined total of ten beds which meet minimum standards of the Mississippi Commission on Hospital Care. In the hospitals incubator babies of both races are

56

kept in the same room, but city and county voters have rejected proposals to construct a Hill-Burton Hospital with state, federal, and local funds for fear it would be integrated.

Not included in the Chamber's brochures is any mention of the strength of the Ku Klux Klan or the more vocal Americans for the Preservation of the White Race. The Klan held a public rally in the spring of 1964 at which Selectman Philip Brady introduced Imperial Wizard Robert Shelton to the assembled Klansmen and their admirers, about seven hundred in all.

McComb lacks the antiquity and the aristocratic antecedents of a Natchez, the midwestern industrial enlightenment of a Tupelo, the cultural eminence and cosmopolitan tolerance of Greenville, the political sights and sounds and odors of Jackson, and the relaxed amorality of Biloxi. The stamp of the roundhouse and the small farm's corn patch bite too deep for any close identification with the older communities in a state which was the twentieth to be admitted to the Union. Pike County, in which McComb lies, is as violent in its past and its present as any in Southwest Mississippi, the state's most turbulent region. Usually the Pike County frontiersmen preferred from the beginning to settle their differences with rifle or pistol or knife and sometimes with all of these. They did not fight by a code duello, demonstrating instead for 150 years a talent for night riding and ambush, for the sudden lunge of a knife to the throat or the back, and a fondness for odds of ten to one in the aggressor's favor.

But most Pike countians are good people, churchgoing,

57

friendly, save when they become suspicious of the stranger. Few of them remain in the frontier tradition, for the railroad, the automobile, and good roads have linked farm to town and town to city and city, so some thought, to the nation. They want their children to go further than they did and not on the farm, for dirt farming is no longer a way of making a decent living. McComb had the first accredited high school in the state. And the county's children have gone far afield by the mounting hundreds to the big cities of the South and the North and are better equipped, though not enough better, than were their fathers, who frequently lacked even a grade-school education.

One seemingly unbreakable thread binds together almost all the white citizens of McComb and Pike County. Until the late autumn of 1964, no other Mississippi county was more united or determined in its resistance to federal civil rights laws. The whites are very serious about this and almost every white citizen is dedicated to the proposition that white and black were created and continue to be unequal, a status to be devoutly maintained as being God's will. Red Heffner likes to tell of the McComb office of Mississippi's Department for the Rehabilitation of the Blind. It has two entrances for the blind people. One door is marked white, the other colored. Red jests that there was talk of having the classification duplicated in Braille on the doorknobs.

The only McComb citizen whose reputation extends beyond the state borders is Oliver Emmerich, the sixty-seven-year-old editor and publisher of the afternoon McComb *Enterprise-Journal*, the county's only daily

58

newspaper, with a circulation of 7000. The *Enterprise-Journal* and Louisiana-born Emmerich, who was a county agent before turning newspaperman forty years ago, have won many journalistic honors. Each year from 1959 to 1965 the Mississippi Press Association has given the paper major awards in its circulation category for general excellence, community service, advertising promotion and editorial achievement. In 1949 the National Editorial Association designated the paper as the one which had been of "greatest service to American agriculture." In 1954 Freedom Foundation gave Emmerich its highest editorial award. What is pertinent here is that in the spring of 1965 his editorials on the McComb conflict won him the editorial award and the *Enterprise-Journal* the distinguished service award given annually by Sigma Delta Chi, the national professional journalistic fraternity; the Sidney Hillman Foundation editorial award; and a citation by the Headliners Club for the best editorials of 1964. For years he has been in demand as a speaker and has appeared frequently outside of the South. Oliver is a kindly, moderate man in a community which considers moderate a dirty word. He has devoted most of his energy to improving what is glibly referred to today as a town's image. He has written eloquently about the need for racial justice and as eloquently about the advantages which his town offers to possible industrial investors and, as a convert to the Republican party, of the need of a two-party system in the state and the South. Time and again his editorials have challenged Mississippi public opinion, though not angrily. More than once he has come to the defense of those few Mississippi editors who more

59

explicitly defy Mississippi conventions. For his pain he
has been buffeted in McComb more often than blessed.
Twice he has been beaten on the streets, once because he
permitted *Life* and *Time* newsmen to use his newspaper
office as their McComb headquarters.

He suffered a light heart attack in 1961. When he had
recuperated sufficiently to reassume the full burden of editorial management, his brilliant only son, John Oliver,
Jr., who is called J.O. or John, a one-time Nieman Fellow
at Harvard and associate editor of the *Enterprise-Journal*, left McComb to become news editor of the Baltimore
Evening Sun.

The Heffners counted Oliver and his gracious wife,
Lyda Will, and J.O. and his wife, Celia, among their
best friends. Carla wrote a witty high school column for
the paper and was J.O. and Celia's favorite baby sitter.
The Heffner family's parakeet is named after the editor.

Late in May, Oliver Emmerich sought to prepare the
people of McComb for the coming of the COFO workers,
which even before their arrival brought his fellow citizens
to a state of mass hysteria.

On May 25 he told the readers of the *Enterprise-Journal* about what he and most other Mississippi editors as
well as others beyond its borders and the South unfortunately labeled "the invasion." It could have better been
described as a Children's Crusade and the effect of no
more than 800 Yankee young people upon 1,100,000 white
Mississippians would have bewildered the fourteenth-
century Saracens who stood manfully against the pitiable
young children who sought to rescue the Holy Land and
died.

The editorial said the demonstrations might start in June, that the young people who were coming would be screened and then trained and the majority would not arrive until July. Emmerich quoted a New York *Times* report which said "some backers of the project are convinced that the student campaigners are seriously motivated, emotionally stable individuals, intent on participating in social change." Their minimum age would be eighteen and if under twenty-one they would have to have written permission from their parents. The editorial related that while most of the workers subscribe to principles of non-violence, others would come prepared to defend themselves.

About the only statement in the editorial that impressed some people, probably a majority, was that an invasion was at hand. Sale of small arms, ammunition, dynamite, and Ku Klux Klan memberships soared to boom proportions.

In the next three editorials Oliver, who had extracted policy statements from the governor, the county sheriff, and the mayor and chief of police of McComb, reassuringly presented their pledges. Their gist was that law and order would be maintained, violence would not be tolerated at any level, and that the unwelcome visitors could sleep soundly. These editorials may have contributed to the fact that the first post-invasion bombing did not take place for almost a month. However, it didn't take Pike and neighboring Amite counties long to catch up with and pass the rest of the state. They had had some practice in home defense. A Catholic attorney for the anti-Catholic Jehovah's Witness sect, which had sought to purchase a church site on the outskirts of town, had recently been told by an alderman that, even if his clients won it wouldn't do any good, as the church would be burned down anyway. The barbershop of the county NAACP leader had been bombed, three nosy Northern journalists had been dragged from their automobile and beaten, and a considerable number of menial Negro employees in white business houses had been fired by popular request. Pike County had also shown up well in a state-wide cross-burning competition.

There were, however, some especially reassuring notes in the third and fourth *Enterprise-Journal* editorials. The sheriff promised that, should people come to the court-house to register, every effort would be made to expedite such procedures with order and decorum. Mayor Gordon Burt said: "I believe that anyone who is qualified to vote should be able to vote. No demonstrations need be held to prove the point. No effort will be made to impede the efforts of anyone seeking to register in the city." These statements must have given the COFO vanguard an early sense of achievement. If the sheriff and the mayor felt this way, they shared with them a common American purpose.

Oliver's final editorial of the series emphasized that the law officers of the state, county, and city were ready for any eventuality. He made an appeal which deserved a far better reception than it received. Oliver spoke hopefully to his neighbors:

"In this series of editorials the *Enterprise-Journal* has sought to inform our people. If there is an invasion of civil rights demonstrators this summer our people will not be caught off-guard. The information published in this newspaper has made known the policies and plans our law enforcement officials will use in the event of a summer invasion.

"It is highly significant that Gov. Paul Johnson at the state level, Sheriff R. R. Warren at the county level and Mayor Gordon Burt and Police Chief George Guy at the city level are all in agreement as to the procedures to pursue.

"No one can reasonably argue that this program of our officials is unfair.

"Gov. Paul Johnson said, 'Individuals who do not infringe upon the rights of others will not be molested or interfered with. If they stand in line they can stand in line as long as they wish provided they do not interfere with the rights of others. But individuals who impede the normal operations of society will be whisked off to jail.'

"Mayor Gordon Burt said, 'In enforcing the law we will see to it that we ourselves observe the law.'

"Said Sheriff R. R. Warren, 'The people must realize that the enforcement of the law must be trusted in the hands of experienced and trained law enforcement officers. We cannot tolerate anyone taking the law into his own hands.'

"Glen Fortenberry, Pike County circuit clerk, advised the *Enterprise-Journal* that he can give the test for voter registration to three applicants at one time. He said, 'We have 10 cards with questions regarding the Constitution. Each applicant, white or colored, can pick any one card from 10. My responsibility is to apply the law and I will apply it to white and colored people alike and with no distinction because of race.'

"These official expressions indicate the determination to pursue a policy of fair play.

"But anyone who, himself, disregards the rights of others or who violates the law will be arrested and placed in jail.

"Now what about us—the people—those of us who are not law enforcement officers?

"Our choice is quite simple: We can be smart or we can be out-smarted.

"Our people could become emotional and panic. We could even resort to mob action and with extreme hysteria find federal troops in our community.

"If this should happen it would prove that we were not smart but rather that we were out-smarted.

"It is necessary that Negro people, as well as white people, relax under the pledge of protection under the law.

"'Freedom Schools' have been announced for this summer. Negroes will be instructed in Mississippi voting laws in these schools. Also announced are plans for Negro people to seek voter registration.

"We repeat for all of our people to know: Gov. Paul Johnson, Sheriff R. R. Warren, Mayor Gordon Burt, Chief of Police Guy, all insist that legal rights of all people will be upheld and that no one has reason for apprehension when operating in a peaceful manner. But if anyone is looking for trouble and ignores the rights of other people, then these law enforcement officers insist that they will tolerate no infringement of the law.

"With the assurance of our elected officials that

64

they are prepared to meet any situation which may arise, the cue for the rest of us is to relax.

"The *Enterprise-Journal* believed it to be the responsibility of this newspaper to fully explore the plans made to meet possible emergencies this summer. The odds are that there will be an invasion of civil rights workers and that most of them will be college students from the North, East and West.

"We have now explored the situation. We know what is planned by outsiders. We know how our own officials plan to cope with what may happen. And we have passed this information along to our readers.

"Our conclusion is that we should all try to relax. Let the law enforcement officers handle the situation for us. They are willing. They stand committed. They insist that they are prepared. What more could we ask?

"May we on Sept. 1 look back on the summer of 1964 and be able to truthfully say, 'We met a crisis with maturity. We did not panic. We exercised restraint. We upheld the dignity of the law. We met a challenge intelligently.'

"If we can say this on Sept. 1 then we will know that we successfully stood the test; that we proved ourselves to be smart, and that we were not outsmarted."

That editorial was the last in quite a spell—the three months of the long, hot summer in fact, *the* period in which some thirty church burnings occurred—on the topic which was the only one discussed anywhere in those late spring days in McComb. Oliver had said everything he knew how to say, he had reasoned with his readers, he

65

had given them facts which should have reassured them. With the advent of the first COFO workers, blind emotionalism gripped the area. Reason had no validity and editorials addressed to reason would make no impression. Oliver's enemies and some of his friends said that Oliver started running scared in June. Certainly he was physically afraid, as would be anyone but a congenital idiot if he has more than once been promised a bomb through his bedroom window and been actually beaten on the streets. But Oliver Emmerich has been threatened before and those warnings had not stilled his editorial voice. In the summer of 1964 there seemed no way to make the voice of reason heard, but as soon as he thought the time had come he struck again. It didn't come soon enough to do the Heffners, who were his friends then, and are now, any good.

In May most people in McComb preferred more exciting reading matter, heady stuff having to do with the preservation of Southern womanhood and the white race, the Communistic Supreme Court, and who wants their daughter to marry a nigger anyhow?

But Oliver's editorial had at least one endorser. Red Heffner, Episcopal lay reader, home-town booster, a damn good salesman, and the best charcoal broiler in town.

At the beginning of the summer of 1964, McComb was a community hag-ridden by fear, fear of a skirmish line of Northern students coming to spread foolish notions about civil rights and to plant seeds of insurrection in the heads of the good darkies of the city and Pike County and Southwest Mississippi; fear of the federal government and the all-seeing agents of the Federal Bureau of Investigation; fear of what might happen next anywhere; fear of the Ku Klux Klan; fear of economic disaster for the individual and for the town. This must be understood if what happened to the Heffners is to be understood. Through the long days and longer nights most of the people of McComb mourned, but not openly, over the bombings and the burnings and the beatings which destroyed the once attractive image of their town. The perpetrators were but a handful. But those who did nothing about it made up, until the leaves of autumn began to fall, all but a tiny fraction of the citizenry. The Heffners' tragedy was a personal one. The larger tragedy and the shame of it were McComb's.

The fear must also be understood if one is to believe in the very existence of a preposterous organization for self-defense against invasion, Help, Inc., to which most of the families of Carroll Oaks and Westview subdivisions belong. The first president was an employee of the Mississippi Adjutant General's office as one of the permanent personnel of the local National Guard unit. Only the Heffners and three or four other families did not join.

Help, Inc. had a set of rules or bylaws or directions which are all that is needed to introduce though not to dismiss the organization. If anyone smiles at the directive, and many have and will, it should be remembered that many also smiled thirty years ago at those Germans who fell in behind a posturing little Austrian with a funny mustache who also postulated dangers and enemies and how to deal with them. By these words in the covering letter which was sent to the families, along with the so-called Guidelines, shall the self-helpers of Carroll Oaks and Westview be known:

"Help, Inc.

"A Community Service Organization

"June 29, 1964

"Dear Neighbor:

"Help, Inc. is an organization of Carroll Oaks and Westview Subdivisions. Its purpose is to better neighborhood relations by getting everyone acquainted with his neighbor around the block and a couple of streets down, not just your immediate neighbors. Also, Help, Inc., is concerned for the dignity of one's privacy, protection of one's family, home and property. We do not consider ourselves alarmists, but we do want to keep the neighborhood alert. Your organization is presently installing an alarm system in the event of any accident, sudden sickness, or any other trouble. More information will be published on this in weeks to come.

"Enclosed you will find Guidelines for self-protection and family protection. These Guidelines are published by your neighborhood organization with the intent of keeping our neighborhood alert to any possible dangers. They are NOT intended to alarm anyone or to instill fear in our families. We hope that this will be emphasized to all concerned.

"Enclosed also is a list of your officers and block captains. If you have any questions about the organi-

zation or guidelines, please do not hesitate to ask
any of the officers or block captains.

"We solicit any suggestions on how we may improve
and promote HELP, INC. Thank you.

Harold A. Crain,
President"

"GUIDELINES FOR SELF-PROTECTION AND PRESERVATION
OF FAMILY PRIVACY

1. Attend block meetings and follow instructions
of Block Captain.

2. Work with your neighbors. Learn entrances and
exits to their homes. Learn locations of bedrooms
used.

3. Offer services to assist neighbor in distress.

4. Know where small children are at all times. If
anything suspicious arises have them come indoors.
Children should go to nearest home—notify parents
if neighbors' children are at your home. Also lock
doors and windows upon hearing alarm.

5. Learn alarm codes. Do not publicize outside
organization.

6. Keep inside during darkness or during periods
of threats.

7. Look before unlocking door to anyone. If suspicious call neighbor or comply with instructions of
Block Captains.

8. Allow no-one to enter unless you know them or
that you are sure their intentions are honorable.

9. Learn all neighbors. Strive for mutual understanding and cooperation.

10. Report any suspicious incident to Block Captain or Assistant.

11. If threatened and an unknown person enters home, try to get to a bedroom, bathroom, or other room where you may lock yourself in.

12. If you are suspicious of impending actions turn all outside lights on. Keep inside lights off. Observe in all directions. If trapped inside any particular room flash light on-and-off repeatedly. Use telephone to get assistance if possible. If telephone is out, resort to signals developed by Block Captains.

13. Learn to remember details. Remember descriptions of persons, what they look like, weight, complexion, hair, clothes, and any other pertinent data. Get description and license numbers of suspicious autos.

14. Prohibit small children from answering door, but rather teach them to look first, then call an adult.

15. If called by neighbor or Block Captain, report to the place of distress and follow instructions of Block Captains.

16. Be suspicious of all strangers until they prove themselves otherwise.

17. Don't try to be a "hero." Ask for help. Numbers discourage.

18. If desired, procure a tear gas pencil or other automatic dispenser.

19. Do not stand by and let your neighbor be assaulted. Assist him with all your means.

20. Be cautious. Prepare yourself mentally and physically.

21. Remain calm. Exercise restraint.

22. Watch your neighbor's house when he is out of town.
23. Lock all access to power supply and circuit breakers.
24. Do not investigate any suspicious acts or noise without adequate lighting at night or without summoning help.
25. Provide outside lights out of immediate reach.
26. Provide adequate locks on doors—chain type locks provide excellent protection.
27. Advise children to be aware of the possibility of being picked up by strangers.
28. Temporary alarm to be three blasts from a shotgun or car horn. . . ."

Help, Inc. had its first chance to show its worth in front of the Heffner home the night of July 17, even before it had completed its organizational process. Two days later Red Heffner's landlord would give him notice to vacate his office by the end of the month. He would neither sell a single policy nor even be able to talk to a single local McComb prospect. Anonymous telephone callers would curse and threaten him and mutter obscenities to the women of the household more than 350 times. Only three of their McComb friends, two of them older women, would cross their threshold, though they visited occasionally in two other homes and talked by telephone to a half-dozen friends. And rumor piled upon vile rumor, day by day, and night by night.

But Falstaff, the dachshund, would be the only member of the family circle to die. Sometime in the night of August 18 he would be struck by a person unknown across

71

the back and left partially paralyzed. He would improve and then he would die mysteriously. So would the cats belonging to the Hallins, the friends who lived across the street, and the Hayes Lees, whose masters also had not accepted membership in Help, Inc.

CHAPTER IV

The intruding COFO white and Negro civil rights workers and the Negro churchgoers of Pike County and elsewhere in Mississippi were the first to feel the summer's withering fury. Before its end, the moldering bodies of the three young COFO members were found where their murderers had hidden them for what they thought would be for all time. Before its end, the ashes of some fifty Mississippi Negro churches had long since grown cold. Before its end, scores of white and Negro challengers of the status quo had been beaten and many had been jailed on charges which were almost laughable, among them the failure to have a food handler's license to prepare food in their own headquarters for themselves and their friends and "criminal syndicalism," an offense for which no one in the United States had been arrested since prior to World War I. Before its end, McComb would have come close to being placed under martial law. Before its end, the Heffners would have suffered more lastingly, save for the three dead boys, than any others who were its victims, for they had been destroyed

73

economically and socially in the town which had been their home for ten years and in the state in which they were born and raised. And, after its end, shaken by a belated recognition of the enormities they had condoned by their silence, approved or remained indifferent to, some 650 white citizens of McComb and Pike County would issue a signed statement calling for an end to anarchy and a public recognition of the fact that the law of the land requires equal treatment and color blindness in its application.

On Saturday morning, July 18, Malva and Red lay late in bed almost disbelieving what had happened the night before. They had not slept much. They told each other that the nightmare was bound to end almost as quickly as it had begun. When Red went to town for his mail, people spoke to him but the glances of some were unmistakable. He heard that an attempt to burn another Negro church the night before had been unsuccessful and that a black powder bomb had been found.

Soon after midday Chief Guy came to the house. He said there was nothing he could do and that the people in Carroll Oaks were in a state of hysteria. Some of the Help, Inc. folk had told him at police headquarters that the only reason the Heffner home had been surrounded and the two COFO workers and the Smiths followed was to protect Sweeney and McCord from bodily injury.

The Heffners had been told the night before that an FBI agent would get in touch with them the next day for a more complete report on the telephone calls. When none showed up, Red phoned and made a definite appointment with an agent to meet him after church the next day.

In the afternoon they visited Miss Allie B. Guy, the police chief's cousin, a parakeet lover, who was keeping Oliver, Carla's parakeet, while Carla was in New York. Oliver and Miss Guy seemed glad to see them.

For the first time in many a month the Heffners neither had company nor went out on a Saturday night. Early in the evening Red telephoned "Bo" Statham, Senator Stennis' assistant, from the pay station at the Illinois Central depot, because he was convinced his phone was tapped, and told him what had happened the night before and asked for advice. And that night the anonymous harassment calls began.

At about two in the morning Malva awakened from a fitful sleep and walked nervously around inside the house. Pausing at the breakfast-room window, she looked out and saw a parked car and the glow of cigarettes inside. She roused Red but he refused to share her anxiety and said the parkers must be some kids at the Elliotts' coming in from a date. Malva became more irritated with Red when he went to the kitchen for a glass of buttermilk and thereby disclosed through the light from the opened refrigerator that someone in the house was awake.

The next morning Red and Malva went to services at the Church of the Mediator. After church the FBI agent with whom the appointment had been made came by. Over a cup of coffee he described in detail the unexploded black powder bomb which had been found under the Negro church and questioned them about what had happened on Friday night.

75

After lunch Red and Malva went to the Holiday Inn where they watched an exhibition of gymnasts. The performers had come in from their training camp just outside of town, one of four in the nation at which gymnasts were training for the Olympics. Malva stayed on for a swim and Red went home to write some letters.

When he returned to the Holiday Inn to pick up Malva, he found her very frightened. Harry Raddon, the manager, had told her that the state highway patrolmen in McComb had heard a rumor that the Heffner house was going to be bombed.

Now Red became greatly alarmed over their personal safety. The report tied in with the figures sitting in the parked car in the darkness of the night before.

Red went immediately to the FBI headquarters on the second floor. He asked the agent who had been at his house whether the FBI had the same tip. The agent replied that they had and he had assumed that the Heffners knew about it also. As Red was leaving the room, the telephone rang. The call was from Don McCord who had also just heard the report. When told that Red was in the suite, Don asked to speak to him. He offered to send some of the SNCC group to help guard the house but Red refused. If somebody was to get hurt, he wanted to do the hurting himself because, while he would have a perfect right to defend his home, he wasn't sure of the status of any volunteer guards.

That night Malva slept at the Holiday Inn and Red, a loaded shotgun and pistol beside his bed, stayed at the house. At midnight and again at three, by prearrangement, someone from COFO headquarters phoned to wake him so that he could check the premises.

This was a turning point in the lives of the Heffners. For the first time they were receiving help from outsiders, the young people at the Freedom House and their advisers. The next morning Don McCord told the Heffners that the Negroes of McComb were looking upon Red as a champion and that if something happened to the house or to them he doubted that the Negroes could be controlled.

Jan returned that day from her grandmother's. She was to participate in the afternoon in a Little League parade in Magnolia and asked wryly if she should have a bullet-proof bubble installed on her convertible. "Mr. Kennedy, after all, had friends in Dallas," she added.

The harassment calls picked up that day. Somehow they didn't come on Sunday—ever. But obviously things weren't blowing over. Yet what had Red done to upset the community so much? He was convinced that if only people knew what he was trying to do, most would agree that he was acting in the interests of all.

Oliver Emmerich made a suggestion which Red seized upon. Why not publish a statement in the *Enterprise-Journal* explaining his position exactly? But when he went by the newspaper office the editor and Red agreed to give the situation a little longer to cool off, without publicity, if it would. However, they worked up a tentative draft of a statement. While Red was in the office, Mayor Burt came in on unrelated business of his own. Red asked the mayor if he would like to sit in on the preparation of his statement but Burt declined.

Jan and Malva slept at the Holiday Inn at Red's insistence. Harry Raddon, nervous about their being there, asked them not to leave their room so as not to be seen by the guests. One heavy-set salesman asked Raddon where the "nigger-loving" Heffner family lived as he wanted to know.

Jonah Ford drove up from Magnolia to stay with Red at the house for several hours. He wanted to be with his friend whom he knew to be in trouble. Except for this personal relationship, Jonah, a thin-faced intellectual, was interested in what was happening in Mississippi more as an academic observer than as a participant. He had found his few contacts with the civil rights workers stimulating. But he certainly did not consider himself any more a part of the civil rights movement than did Red and Malva.

When he returned to Magnolia and went to the all-night service station across from his mother's nursery to buy a pack of cigarettes, he was told that another church had been burned. He telephoned Red who notified the FBI.

The notice to Red evicting him from his office came by registered mail the next morning. His friend, "Pooley" Alford, could have telephoned him. The letter was brief and pointed.

> Dear Red:
> I will need the office space you are now occupying in the Alford Building August 1st, and I am sorry I will have to ask you to give it up prior to that time.
> Yours very truly,
> Pooley
> Julius M. Alford

78

Malva and Jan left Tuesday for Vicksburg, where Jan's successor as Miss Mississippi was to be chosen.

That night the anonymous calls again increased in number and viciousness.

"If you want to live, get out of town."

"How does your wife like sleeping with niggers?"

"You nigger-loving bastard."

"You're going to get your teeth kicked in."

"What window do you want the bomb in?"

Sharing the evening with Red were Jonah and several young friends of Carla's who asked him what had really happened and told him some of the rumors which were going around.

Red says that if the heavens fell in he would still find himself transporting dresses his womenfolk had forgotten. Wednesday was no different in this respect from many other days. Before leaving to join Malva and Jan in Vicksburg, Red had to go by the dressmaker to pick up the gowns she had made for Jan. She too had been hearing rumors. Mrs. Newman didn't know the family too well and confused what she had heard about Jan's father with Red. She asked, "Mr. Heffner, aren't you from somewhere up North?" He had the happy satisfaction of answering, "Yes, mam. From north Greenwood."

Of more consequence, he went to the *Enterprise-Journal* to revise his statement, which he had decided he had to run. Up to this time there had been no mention of any kind in newspapers or on radio or television about what was happening to the Heffners. Red's statement was the first disclosure in print. It was intended for his

79

fellow citizens. This was a matter to be settled by Mc-Comb people in McComb. The story as it appeared read:

"It has been reported generally that some civil rights workers were entertained in my home Friday evening. It is true that two white civil rights workers were in my home on this evening. But it was a conference and not a matter of entertainment. The purpose of the conference was to let the civil rights workers hear the Mississippi point of view.

"Nothing was done in my home or elsewhere which was not fully disclosed to law enforcement authorities at the time. I have worked closely with the authorities for the best interests of our town and state. I shall always work to this end for each and every member of my family is a native Mississippian, dedicated to the best interest of our people."

CHAPTER V

Tuesday marked the beginning of the festivities in Vicksburg which would close Jan's year as Miss Mississippi. Starting with a parade that night in which rode some fifty girls representing Mississippi towns, cities, and colleges, each evening through Saturday they would display their talents, poise, beauty, and intellects. From their number a new Miss Mississippi would be chosen.

After dropping Jan at the Hotel Vicksburg where she, as Miss Mississippi, would stay with the other girls, Malva went on to the Vicksburg Holiday Inn where the Heffners had reservations. There she telephoned, at Angela Smith's suggestion, Angela's good friend Mrs. Robert Allen, wife of an Episcopal minister in town. Mrs. Allen spent part of the afternoon with Malva and took her to lunch the next day. She and her husband showed a most sympathetic interest in the Heffners' pyramiding plight and comforted Malva.

But when Red arrived in Vicksburg he found Malva extremely nervous. Something else had happened.

A newspaperman from the Chicago *Daily News*, a

Nick Von Hoffman, had learned through COFO workers what was happening to the family, she said, and had telephoned from Jackson to request an interview. She hadn't known what to do. Von Hoffman seemed to know so much of the story. What could she do to stop him from using it? She didn't want it to come out and mar Jan's last days as Miss Mississippi and, in any case, it would further damage the state's reputation. She hadn't been able to talk to Red, who was already on the road from McComb. She had asked Von Hoffman not to come to the Holiday Inn until Red would have time to arrive and talk to him.

During the two hours before Red arrived at the motel she had tried to reach Governor Paul Johnson, she said. He would tell her what to do. He was an old friend of the Coopers'. When her father died, Paul Johnson's gold chrysanthemum horseshoe was the largest floral offering at the funeral. He had been in Vicksburg dedicating a power plant. But when she talked to a secretary in Mayor John Holland's office she had learned that he had already left for an engagement in Greenville. As Malva saw it, this was an emergency in which the good name of the state was at stake and she said so. She asked to talk to the mayor, who had been with the Heffners at many pageant functions in the past year. Holland came to the motel at once. He advised Malva to evade any questions Von Hoffman might ask.

When Red arrived, she still had not given the newspaperman an interview although he was now at the motel.

Red settled the matter by talking with Von Hoffman

at length. But they agreed before he began that every-thing he said would be off the record and that Nick would not write anything about the Heffners unless Red told him it was all right to do so. Red emphasized that the Heffners lived in McComb and wanted to live there and a story would only aggravate the situation. Red found Nick a reasonable, friendly, and perceptive man who understood the situation and kept the requested promises.

That was the first night of the Miss Mississippi Pageant and Jan graced the stage at the Municipal Auditorium, as she would each night for the rest of the week. The Reverend Stephen Wood, connected with All Saints Episcopal Junior College and a member of the sponsoring Junior Chamber of Commerce, was backstage each evening and kept a close watch over her in case the tension of the family trouble would cause her to break.

Thursday, Red drove to Jackson for a conference with Erle Johnston. Johnston listened to Red's recital of what was happening to the Heffners, but offered no solution. No one in authority seemed to show much concern. Red returned to Vicksburg and, to the extent that his anxiety permitted, enjoyed the spectacles of the remaining three nights of the pageant and Jan's participation in it.

On the final night of her reign as Miss Mississippi, Jan's Grandmother Cooper came from Forest, Brother Wilson drove from Jackson, and another beau, Eugene Howard, the son of the mayor of Monroe, Louisiana, also was on hand to hear her gracious farewell before removing the crown from her own head and placing it on that of the new Miss Mississippi. It is the most dramatic moment in the annual pageant.

The next day Jan went to her grandmother's for a rest, something Red and Malva could not guarantee her if she returned home. As for them, they went to McComb by way of Jackson and a night with friends there. Red hoped to have a chance to talk to Auburn Lambeth, the Lincoln National Life general agent, on Monday. Lambeth had probably heard some of the rumors and Red wanted to give his superior and friend a true account. Red learned Monday morning Lambeth was in Atlanta. So, leaving Malva to follow later, he drove to McComb alone.

When he walked into the house the phone was ringing. The caller was a civil rights attorney who asked to see him. Not wishing to have anyone at his home in the daytime who would seem suspicious to his neighbors, Red suggested that they meet at the Church of the Mediator. Never before had he refused to let anyone come to his home. More significantly, it represented a subconscious effort to conform.

That day's edition of the *Enterprise-Journal* contained a bombshell for the Heffners. Red had been confident that his statement in the Wednesday paper would straighten things out for him. But today the sheriff issued a statement of his own which completely cut the ground from under Red's. Sheriff Warren said that Red had not talked with him. The sheriff was right. Red had telephoned the sheriff's home, but Warren was out and Red had not called again. He believes that his failure to

84

do so and the sheriff's statement did more to destroy him in McComb than anything else.

Jonah came to commiserate. No one else sought the Heffners' company. But at least some people knew they were home. The harassment calls began again.

And Red learned from the Hallins that while he was away the Help, Inc. neighbors had taken shifts guarding the house. The rumors about the Heffners had become so widespread and incendiary—a good word for the spirit of McComb in the summer of 1964—that they feared a bombing which might damage their own property.

The next day Red managed despite his depression to complete some pension-plan data for Gulf States Theatres with whose management he had been working since early summer.

On Tuesday morning Dee Morgan, who had never been in the Heffner home before, popped her head in to ask Malva to come over the next day to have coffee with a mutual friend who had returned for a short visit to McComb. Dee was the first adult McCombite to enter the house in eleven days. But that afternoon Red and Malva learned how complete their ostracism was to be. Harry Raddon phoned and asked them apologetically not to visit him at the inn any more.

Wednesday night Jonah and Mrs. Price had supper with them. That day Mrs. Price had sat in on a Civil Rights Commission meeting for the first time and had heard the testimony of a number of Negroes who told graphically of the ways their civil rights had been curtailed. She was emotionally fatigued by the experience

85

and what she had to say was not encouraging to the Heffners.

Red went to Jackson the next day to talk things over with Lambeth. He found him most understanding and co-operative. But Red was becoming more and more worried about whether they would be able to keep their head above water. He went to Senator Stennis' Jackson office in the Post Office Building to talk with Marx Huff, the senator's chief administrative aide. There he picked up some Form 57s, the application for federal employment. Already Dennis Sweeney had written his family's friend, Senator Wayne Morse of Oregon, to ask him to recommend Red to former Governor LeRoy Collins of Florida for a job in the new Community Relations Service, of which President Johnson had appointed Collins director. Red realized that Mississippi's senators could not assist a man as "controversial" as he had become or help place him in a bureau of which they could not publicly approve. But, clutching at straws, he hoped he could somehow get a job less dependent on local popularity.

After Red returned from Jackson, Don McCord telephoned from Freedom House to say that the Right Reverend Paul Moore, Jr., Episcopal Suffragan Bishop of Washington, D.C. was in town and wanted to meet the Heffners. With a feeling of humiliation because he had virtually to smuggle a bishop of his church into his home, Red drove to the Church of the Mediator to pick up the clerical visitor.

Other guests also gathered at the Heffners' that night. Earlier, Red had invited three FBI agents, and Jan, who

86

was home from Forest, had several friends in, including Gene Howard. His Louisiana license and the out-of-state tag on the FBI car were too much for the watchdogs of Help, Inc. Once again the vigilantes began encircling the house. One of the agents seated with his back to the picture window very obviously felt uncomfortable in so vulnerable a spot.

Shortly the circling cars drove away. Evidently someone had recognized the FBI automobile.

But it was not an uneventful night.

The Heffners say that the towering bishop, broad-shouldered and six foot five, whom they would later refer to as the Big Fisherman, gave them that night much of the spiritual strength they would need for the ordeal ahead.

CHAPTER VI

The Heffners became the scapegoats for a community's hysteria, bigotry, ignorance, cowardice, and fear, which in time of unfamiliar stress form a scum which hides whatever bubbles cleanly in the human cauldron.

Saturday, August 1, was a day of especial sadness. Red moved out of his office. He returned to the Oldsmobile agent the convertible which Jan had been using during her year of glory through the courtesy of the Oldsmobile Company. And he received a disapproving and worried letter from his mother.

But there was also a pathetic hopefulness in Red's diary entries at the beginning of the last month in which he and Malva and their daughter would live in McComb.

"Sunday morning. The congregation seemed very friendly today. . . . Some of Jan and Carla's friends seem to be worried . . .

"Monday morning. Rags Watkins came by this morning to visit. He is the first adult McComb visitor that we have had for a real visit other than Colton and Angela since this whole thing started. . . . I ran into Lit

Alford in the Post Office and he did speak cordially. The anonymous calls have fallen off. People must be getting tired. I wish some gal without a husband would get pregnant so they'd have something else to talk about."

"But we were coming close to the breaking point," Red said afterward. "Almost no friends, a few kid friends of the girls, no business, no way to answer the filthy rumors that Jonah and a couple of others told us about. People were saying Carla was really attending a Communist training school in New York. The company had fired me for dishonesty. I was on the payroll of the NAACP. Our coming to McComb was all a part of a Communist conspiracy and I had been planted there ten years ahead. Malva and I were breaking up. Jan was a tipster for the FBI. Malva was a call girl at the Holiday Inn. Jan was going to leave us. Malva had been giving away pictures of herself in the nude. That was the damnedest one of all. Any husband with a Polaroid camera and a good-looking wife usually gets the two together. And I had taken a picture of her a few years before without much on. A reporter whom I let look over a drawerful of war-atrocity photographs found the picture in the drawer and palmed it. We had forgotten it was there. When things got rough he started showing it around town just before he left for another job."

The sexual innuendoes were not really important. Had Mary Magdalen or the Virgin Mary been in McComb, Mississippi, in the stead of Mary Alva Heffner they would have been given the same treatment. That was the way it was.

But a man has to go through the motions. No individual clients would see him, but Red kept calling on his industrial and other pension-plan prospects. Now and then came happy interludes. Pete Seeger, the folk singer who was in Mississippi to do what he could for the civil rights movement, telephoned from COFO headquarters and sang a song for Jan and sent her his autograph, which was brought by two white McComb youngsters who had dared to go to the Freedom House to hear him sing.

In one diary entry Red noted his worry over money. His usual commission check was delayed through a clerical error in Fort Wayne.

Because he still hoped that somehow the Heffners could stay in Mississippi, he declined to give a story to a religious news-service reporter and to *Newsweek*, but he did make a tape in the parish house for a representative of the Canadian Broadcasting Company on the broad topic of Mississippi's reaction to the student invaders. Nick Von Hoffman was keeping his promise not to release anything unless Red gave him permission.

For Malva the days were as dreary as they were heartbreaking. Red managed to keep himself busy. Mostly he wrote letters, but few of the letters had anything to do with insurance. After his once-a-day trip to the post office he stayed at the typewriter he had moved from the downtown office building. Malva played solitaire in her bedroom and cooked the meals that neither of them felt like eating. Now and then a friend phoned, but not often. When she kept her once-a-week appointment at the beauty parlor, the operator was friendly but few of the customers were.

All this time, which was no time at all, being less than three weeks, something was happening to the Heffners of which at first they were only dimly aware. Their economic and perhaps physical security gone and their community status as low as that of the COFO young people whose paths they had innocently tried to smooth for the good of the community and the interlopers alike, the Heffners found themselves becoming aligned in a way that they would not have dreamed of at the beginning of the summer. Shunned by almost everyone they knew in McComb, they entered upon a forced voyage of discovery of other people, the assortment of outsiders, students and lawyers and doctors and sociologists and ministers who had not come to Mississippi to make a living but, as they saw it, to help. It was the sort of help that white Mississippi didn't welcome. In New York young Carla had similarly discovered part of her of which she had been unaware, a part which has to do with certain values: justice, a sense of the right of any human being to dignity and self-respect, the need for brotherhood among men, the courage and idealism that could cause teenagers to face up to the policeman's billy, the nauseous small-town jail cells, and at the ultimate a roaring .45. Fatuous? Not in McComb that summer.

"At first we were pushed into it," Malva believes. "After all, the people we thought were our friends ran from us as though we were contagious lepers. Those who stuck with us were people like Dennis Sweeney and Don McCord and later those Episcopal priests in Jackson and the Yankee newspapermen. We were lonely and they came and we learned from them. It feels now as if something heavy has been taken off our back."

Suddenly, through the catalyst of Bishop Moore's presence in their home, they had seen their problem as definitely and simply and prosaically a question of right and wrong. From the evening of his visit on, they knew that they could not do public penance for their local heresy in breaking Mississippi's code of hate and fear of "outsiders" advocating racial and social change.

Not every aspect of this transition was serious. Late in July Red had received a long-distance call from Jimmy Bostick, a former Edsel dealer in McComb who had moved with his family to Baton Rouge. Off and on during the time that Bostick had lived in McComb he and Red had talked of the possibility of going into business together. Now Jimmy Bostick was ready. He had heard of Red and Malva's difficulties through their across-the-street neighbors Pete and Helen Hallin. He suggested that they form a partnership in Baton Rouge. They arranged a meeting in Hammond, Louisiana, a halfway point between McComb and Baton Rouge.

The Bosticks and the Heffners had a pleasant reunion in Hammond. They talked enthusiastically of the venture. But Red would need some money. There was none in sight unless he could close the Gulf States pension plan and sell the house. Neither that insurance program nor any other then in sight came through, and the house was not sold for many months.

Fifteen miles south of Hammond lies Pass Manchac, which connects Lake Maurepas and Lake Pontchartrain, above New Orleans. It is known for its rustic seafood cafes. Just before their conference with the Bosticks, Malva and Red telephoned Dennis Sweeney and Don McCord to ask that they meet them in Hammond and from there drive together to Middendorf's Cafe at Pass Manchac for supper. Red was partial to the fried catfish and hushpuppies there.

Some people can preserve a sense of humor even in the time of worst adversity.

"We were dumbfounded when we reached Middendorf's place over a sign that proclaimed it was a private club," Red says. "It was the first time any of us had seen proof of a way of getting around the civil rights statutes. Us Mississippians aren't used to being turned away from anywhere and so I walked on in. We were promptly seated. We ordered and our orders were filled. But during the meal the waitress brought us some application blanks for ourselves and our friends to join the private club. That gave me an inspiration."

Red's inspiration was to fill out an application for membership in the name of M. (for Martin) L. (for Luther) King. For his own credentials Red flashed an old card identifying him as an honorary deputy sheriff in Scott County, Mississippi. It had expired the preceding January. As his telephone number he gave that of the COFO house in McComb. Red turned over the promptly issued King membership certificate to Sweeney, who was to mail it to the Reverend Mr. King.

The evening was a relaxed one but the relaxation was not permanent. On their way back to McComb they heard on the radio that the bodies of the three missing civil rights workers had been found in Neshoba County.

93

Back in McComb nothing had changed. The next day Red made these entries in his diary:

"Wednesday, August 5.

"Report of another church burning in Adams County.

"Still no mail from Washington or checks. Maude Fitzgerald called. She had the idea that she would like to have Don McCord talk to her Presbyterian Sunday School class. This is encouraging, but we know that Maude does not realize how serious this is. Spoke with Libby Price for a few minutes and had coffee with her. Saw Jonah and spoke with him from the car. He had been down on the Coast. Called on Leon Pickard [the Chevrolet agent in Magnolia] about a key man insurance policy. He seemed very cool. I may be oversensitive about this. . . .

"Spoke with 'Bo' Statham by phone. He acknowledged receipt of Form 57 and letter but seemed to express some doubt as to ability to help with Governor Collins. Also expressed sympathy and concern." Red should have been aware that a great many Mississippians were touting for senator on an independent ticket former Governor Ross Barnett, who had done his best to lead Mississippi out of the Union for a second time. So far Senator Stennis had no declared opposition in the November general election. He wanted to keep it that way.

"Talked with Jim Silver. He very adamantly counseled against Carla's going to school in McComb for her senior year."

Red had no place of business except the den in the house in Carroll Oaks. He had almost no business. Now a pressing family decision must be made. He and Malva

94

told each other that Jim Silver was right. The only answer unless a federal appointment came through seemed to be to move to Jackson where, in the state's largest city, they might enjoy a merciful anonymity for a while, Red could continue with Lincoln National, and Carla could be enrolled in a school where she wouldn't be a marked student. Jan would return to M.S.C.W. But still they kept hoping they could stay in McComb. It was home.

Colton Smith, who was going to be out of town on vacation, left with Red the lay-reader sermon to be given on Sunday. The title, Red says, was apropos: "You Are Not Alone." Later that day, at the suggestion of Jean Jackson, Libby Price's niece whom they had often visited in Jackson, Red talked things over with Joe Pigott, the district attorney for the Pike, Walthall, Lincoln, and Copiah counties' circuit court. They conferred for an hour and a half.

"Joe's suggestion was that I go from house to house in Carroll Oaks and seek some sort of reconciliation with my neighbors. This smacks too much of apologizing for something we are not ashamed of. I can't see myself doing such a thing."

That same day Red read in the *Enterprise-Journal* of the burning of a 100-year-old Negro church in Holmesville in Pike County, not far from McComb. No civil rights meetings had been held in the church. But undeniably it was a Negro church.

In the evening Red and Malva drove down to Magnolia to have supper with Libby Price. While they were there, Jonah Ford brought in an ominous little story. A stranger, one whom he ironically described as a kind friend, had

95

accosted his mother at the family nursery and suggested that the business and the Ford family would both be a lot more secure if Jonah would quit seeing the Heffners.

It was imperative indeed that they talk to Auburn Lambeth at Lincoln National and see if it would be possible for Red to work out of the Jackson office. While he was in the capitol city he would also borrow some money against deferred commissions. And when he got back he would do something about trying to sell their home.

In Jackson Red had no trouble borrowing the $500 from the Deposit Guaranty Bank, which did not ask for security, and he and Malva were welcomed at the Lambeths' home where Auburn touched only briefly but reassuringly on Red's relationship with the company, whether he lived in McComb or Jackson.

As another indication of the new orientation of the Heffners, they decided when they left the Lambeths' to drive the few miles to Tougaloo College where Don McCord was attending a conference. As white Mississippians they had never before thought of inspecting the small, privately endowed, church-supported, and controversial college which was founded for Negroes by Northern Methodist churchmen and philanthropists soon after the end of the Civil War. Its student body, which in a small way is integrated, is almost entirely Negro with a scattering of non-Southern whites. Its president has traditionally been white. The faculty is made up of members of both races on equal footing. Its militancy has been, in recent years, a vexation in Mississippi and the subject of much demagogic discussion.

The Heffners first saw Tougaloo three weeks to the day

96

from the time they served the hot tamales to Dennis Sweeney and Don McCord.

"Malva and I had never before found ourselves in a socially integrated group," Red recalls. "What surprised us most of all was that we didn't feel awkward. We were aware that nobody else seemed ill at ease either. One of the people we met was a Miss Baker, a Negro, whom we had seen on television. She urged us to guard against being bitter toward our neighbors. We were also introduced to Robert Moses and James Foreman, both Negro leaders in the SNCC outfit."

They met others, too, who previously had only been friendly voices on the telephone. One of them, who made a lasting impression, was Father Harry Bowie, a Negro Episcopal priest from Lawnside, New Jersey, and a graduate of the General Theological Seminary in New York. Father Bowie had been a classmate of Colton Smith. Red and Malva were surprised at some of the other white visitors who were there, among them teachers or graduate students from Mississippi and Tennessee.

"It was really something to stand up and talk to people with dark skins man to man without having to look over your shoulder," Red says. "It was like being in a cold shower thirty seconds after you step in. You don't notice the temperature."

Sunday, two days later, was a busy one. With Colton Smith out of town, Red conducted the morning services at both Magnolia and McComb.

"I had invited Don and Dennis to come to Magnolia. I wanted them to hear me read the sermon which I would

97

not be doing in McComb because we were showing a religious movie there instead. After church we went into the parish house and had coffee. Libby Price and I introduced Don and Dennis to most of the congregation. I was very proud of the Magnolia people. They were cordial and no one brought up Topic A. As guests of the church, Don and Dennis were treated with dignity and courtesy. All through the summer white COFO people regularly attended services at the Church of the Mediator, whether they were Episcopalians or not, usually three or four at a time. However, they would leave immediately after services and had no contact with the congregation. I'll always love that little Magnolia church for the way its members treated those two.

"After coffee I drove to the Church of the Mediator and left after I had read morning prayer but before the movie.

"When I got home, I called Don and Dennis to see how they liked the way I conducted the service and the people of the church in Magnolia. Don was almost in tears because of what had happened since I had left them an hour before. When they got back to McComb, he and Dennis had tried to go to the Disciples of Christ Church. Remember, Don is an ordained Disciples of Christ minister. As soon as they entered the building, ushers took each of them by the elbows and escorted them outside."

The next day was more pleasant than most. Red mowed his own lawn, the grass in Shelly Circle in front of his house, and the grounds of Ben Payne, a neighbor who was away on vacation with his family. He didn't want it to be so apparent that the Paynes were gone, he says. He and Malva had lunch with the Emmerichs. Red remembers that he was treated courteously at the First National Bank where he offered his house for sale to Billy Neville, III, the son of the president, before listing it with a realtor. That night the Heffners visited in their room at the Holiday Inn with some friends from Laurel and came home feeling less lonely than they had for a long time.

Before going to bed, Red wrote a letter to Don McCord, who had left Mississippi for his newly assigned pulpit in Minnesota. Red set down an interesting sidelight on the presidential campaign:

"While we were at Tougaloo I casually mentioned that Barry Goldwater, Jr., was to speak at the fair in Neshoba County where the three civil rights boys were murdered," Red says. "A young Negro woman named Marian Wright, who is an attorney for the NAACP Legal Defense Fund, recalled that Northern Negro Republicans had been promised that none of the Goldwaters would speak before segregated audiences in the South and excused herself. When she returned she told us she had sent a wire to somebody or other. I don't remember the name. But the interesting thing is that the appearance was canceled. The excuse was that there had been a foul-up in the speaking schedule."

But Barry Goldwater carried Mississippi more one-sidedly, almost nine to one, than he did any other of the five states which saved him from a shutout.

Those people of McComb who were law abiding, as most of them were, dreaded the coming of night. At night churches were burned and homes dynamited and no one

99

could feel certain that the dynamiters and arsonists wouldn't strike not only at Negroes but at such whites as might stand publicly against the terror. At night-time came the anonymous telephone calls. At night-time the Klan rode and few dared defy its dictates. Crosses were burned in the front yards of Dr. W. T. Mayer and G. T. Vaccarella, Jr. Dr. Mayer had contributed to a fund to rebuild the burned-out churches. Vaccarella, who operates the ShopRite Grocery in McComb, had ignored efforts to force him to discharge Negro employees. Few people were as brave as Mrs. Zeb Fitzgerald who dared to drop in to see the Heffners who until then had been little more than her casual acquaintances. She knew how badly they needed friends.

Red Heffner's ebullience is amazing. The future bleak and meeting one business rebuff after another—one of the larger pension plans he had been working on was turned down—he thought it would be good to have a get-together in New Orleans with those white and Negro COFO workers whom the Heffners knew only as friendly voices on the telephone and who had had precious little recreation of any kind that summer. Many of the young students had never been to New Orleans, and an integrated social evening was impossible for the Heffners in McComb. They wanted no additional danger for themselves or the COFO workers. The only way an integrated party of this kind could be possible in New Orleans as far as Red knew would be for the gathering to be church associated.

Another Episcopal priest contributed, though indirectly, to the Heffners' break with the code.

Father Henry H. Crisler of a prominent Port Gibson,

Mississippi, family, who had prepared Red and Malva for confirmation, is the priest in charge of Saint Anna's, a mission in a blighted area of New Orleans. Father Crisler agreed to let the group meet at his apartment, although he himself would be in Denver.

When the Heffners and Jonah arrived at the rectory that Friday night, the door was opened by a lay reader. Shortly thereafter twelve COFO workers arrived in two cars from McComb. It was interesting to the Heffners actually to see what these people looked like and to hear their versions of shared experiences. Soon it was time to eat. Everything had gone so smoothly that they decided to go out for dinner rather than have a sandwich supper at the rectory. Father Harry Bowie proposed a restaurant that he knew about on Canal Street. He made the reservations.

Perhaps only a white Southerner can comprehend the dramatic quality of Malva's and Red's decision to dine publicly in a Southern city with Negroes.

"It was a very nice restaurant," Red says. "None of us had been there before. We were all treated with dignity. A few people in the bar stared for a while but they finally got tired of it and went back to their drinks. Malva said she saw some people come to the door and turn away. After dinner, Malva and I thanked the manager for his courteous treatment. Then we went back to the rectory and the COFO folks left for McComb. Malva and Jonah and I pub crawled into the early hours."

The Freedom House workers didn't get back to McComb in time for the bombing of a grocery store on the first floor of the Negro Masonic Hall. But they were there

Saturday night when twenty-four regular and auxiliary policemen raided the headquarters on the pretext of searching for illegal whisky and for proof of illegal cohabitation between white and Negro workers. They found no proof of miscegenation. The only spiritous liquor the cops came across was a bottle of sacramental wine which they took to be vinegar. No one was arrested that night, but a young Harvard law student, jailed the night before after the grocery-store bombing, was still in jail waiting for the posting of a $350 bond. He had protested the incident too loudly.

That same Saturday night the Heffners had dinner by prearrangement in New Orleans with McComb friends they had not been with in over a month, though normally they would have been seeing each other frequently. Lorna and Atkins Williams and Malva and Red found it hard to keep the conversation going. It was impossible to discuss the situation which was keeping them apart and nothing else was really worth talking about.

On Sunday night, Ward James, a friend of Carla's, dropped in. He had been at the house about an hour when an anonymous caller warned him to leave the house at once. He did. Throughout the night the telephone kept ringing.

The raid on the COFO headquarters signaled the beginning of the harassment arrests which were to plague the students until the summer's end. But that week Red felt better because his mother, who had learned of the phone tapping and the rest, telephoned to tell him that she was on their side. He and Malva had an amusing letter from Carla saying that she was packed and ready to come home and that she had read and howled over the idiotic rules of Help, Inc. Another cheerful note was contributed by Chief Guy, who told Red that he had stopped the circulation of a petition demanding that the Heffners move out of the neighborhood. Red told the chief that he and Malva would sell the house to the Help, Inc. members if they would chip in to buy it. But there were no takers.

By now the Heffners were meeting more Yankee folk than anybody else in McComb's history. Among them were Dr. Arnold Goldberg, a psychiatrist from Chicago, and Dr. Tom Levin, a New York clinical psychologist; the Reverend John Cannon, an Episcopal chaplain of Columbia University, and the Reverend Eugene Monick, who is an Episcopal priest serving as executive secretary for college work in the Diocese of New York; the Reverend Melvin Van De Workeen, a Unitarian minister; and Jim Millstone of the St. Louis *Post-Dispatch*. The doctors were in Mississippi, together with other Northern physicians, to ascertain whether the civil rights workers could receive adequate medical care from state practitioners. Mississippi's doctors didn't like the inference, for only two of their number, as far as they knew, had not lived up to the oath of Hippocrates. One had not protested the beating of a minister and a COFO worker when they came to his office for treatment. Another had refused to treat a National Council of Churches minister and ordered him out of the office.

In his diary Red noted sardonically that the Red Cross had taken a pint of his blood without question.

Red's notations for Wednesday, August 19, were a miscellany of significant and trivial happenings. This was the morning when Red found Falstaff at the door, obviously injured and in considerable pain. He took him to a veterinarian and was told to exercise him frequently and give him some prescribed tablets, to which he seemed to respond encouragingly. Crosses had been burned in the yards of Circuit Judge William A. Watkins, Jr., who had given a strong charge to the grand jury in Walthall County, and Charles Hughes, master of the McComb Masonic Lodge, an Englishman who spoke his mind publicly. A stink bomb had been exploded in Woolworth's, but only two threatening calls came through to the Heffners'. Their whisky supply was low so Red and Malva drove "down to the line" where, across the Louisiana state line from dry Mississippi, most McCombites who drink make their liquor purchases. On the way back they dropped in for a few minutes with Harry and Sue Case, old friends.

Later Red picked up three Episcopal priests from the Church of the Mediator. They laughed when he told them that, although the Heffners were the senior citizens of Carroll Oaks, they had not been invited to the forthcoming Saturday night covered-dish supper, the first social event sponsored by Help, Inc.

The rest of the week was a hodgepodge of ups and downs, of small satisfactions and of concern over some impractical and even dangerous projects suggested by several of the COFO workers. Red noted happily that he and Malva went across the street to the Hallin home where they enjoyed themselves as they had in the old days a month before, but they were told that, while they were welcome any time, the Hallins themselves didn't think it wise for them to make a return visit.

Ever since the first incident, Malva had been brooding over Oliver Emmerich's failure to come to their defense in the *Enterprise-Journal*. Red himself was disturbed by the tone of news stories written by the *Enterprise-Journal's* top reporter, Charles Gordon. On Thursday night Malva phoned Oliver and "sort of raised hell with him." At Oliver's request, Red went by the next morning, after seeing Malva off to take some clothes to Jan in Forest, and had what he described as "a chat which accomplished nothing."

But Oliver Emmerich was acting in the way he thought best for the Heffners and for McComb.

"Nobody could have gotten through to the people of McComb during the summer," Emmerich says. "Almost everybody was hysterically afraid. I was apprehensive myself. I thought that the fever had to run its course before anything could be done and that Red and Malva were better off without publicity at the time. I could have been wrong. But that's what I honestly believed. We have never consciously failed a friend when we thought we could help him by speaking out. I still believe it wouldn't have helped in July or August in the atmosphere that had been created in McComb."

Friday night, with Malva out of town, Red went alone to a movie theatre where *Cleopatra* was showing and smoked a cigarette at intermission with Ernest Zeeck. Later Zeeck would be one of the first three Pike County men arrested in connection with the church bombings.

Red had planned to spend the weekend in Forest with Malva at the Coopers'. But when Philip Enochs—a member of a prominent Mississippi family and an officer in

105

Fernwood Industries—suggested that Malva and Red and Enochs and his wife, Jackie, go to the country club together Saturday night, he decided it would be better to accept this invitation from friends, especially if he would be seen in public. He did go and enjoyed himself. Playing bingo he won a certificate entitling him to a stuffed-flounder dinner.

By now the young people at the Freedom House were turning increasingly to Red for advice. He was horrified when one of them told him how disappointed they were that a meeting with some fifteen McComb youths in an isolated cabin had failed to develop. He reminded them of Philadelphia. Red wrote that with Dennis home in Oregon, where he was politicking to get the Freedom Democratic party seated at the National Democratic party's convention, "the COFO people seem to be getting a group of green hands and I am very afraid that they are in for increased trouble."

Malva and Jan got back on Monday, August 24. Malva told him that her family couldn't understand why they had become so involved. As for Jan she "seems simply and completely neutral and prefers not to discuss anything."

On that day Red's diary contained one revealing comment which would have confirmed everything the people of McComb were thinking of him. Of the visiting doctors, ministers, social workers, and lawyers from the North who were linked one way or another with the Mississippi Summer Project, he wrote: "I am constantly amazed by the competence and stature of these people. I wish McComb could realize this."

CHAPTER VII

While Red was enjoying himself at the Country Club Saturday night with the Enochs, Help, Inc. was holding its first pot-luck supper.

The *Enterprise-Journal* covered the event, which was graced by the presence of the mayor:

"An estimated 200 persons or more turned out Saturday night for a community-wide pot-luck supper in Carroll Oaks and Westview subdivisions.

"The affair was sponsored by Help, Inc., a community organization and was attended by residents of the community and invited guests. It was held on a vacant lot at the corner of Wilson and Gerald drives.

"Entertainment during and after dinner was provided by the Starlighters and the Camellia City Quartet. Sheriff R. R. Warren gave the invocation, and Charlie Stringer was master of ceremonies.

"The food, served buffet style, was provided by those who attended, with persons from different streets bringing different dishes.

"Harold Crain is president of Help, Inc."

Early the following week Jonah, who to protect his mother had been careful not to leave his car parked in front of the Heffner home, drove right up to the house. He had come to say goodbye. He was leaving for a year's study of medieval theology at the University of Edinburgh. The Heffners knew they would feel the absence of this loyal friend.

But Thursday night the family circle was complete. Carla arrived home. Malva, Red, and Jan drove to New Orleans to meet her, going first to dinner at Brennan's and then putting Dr. Tom Levin, who had driven down with them, on a plane for New York. Carla said she wasn't too sure what she was coming home to but, whatever it was, she was glad to be there.

The next day Carla had a sampling of what home meant now. Almost every place she went someone jeeringly called her Miss COFO, even in the Youth Center. In the afternoon she received the first of the obscene phone calls that would be directed at her. While many of her friends dropped by to welcome her home, the parents of her best friend gave orders that the girl could not go to the Heffners'.

But there was more cause for tears that Saturday.

"One of the saddest days I ever spent. Falstaff died," Red's diary reads. "He had been O.K. and suddenly, when Carla returned with cokes, he was dead in the front yard. We buried him by Fellow. Did not believe it possible to become so attached to a little dog. He was about the finest little dog a family could have. He loved us all without asking anything but to be with us. Such love and loyalty is rare, even in a dog."

The family sodded the grave the next day and Malva cried almost all that night and the next. Helen Hallin and Maxine Lee also had cause to cry because they found their cats dead in their own yards. It won't hurt to repeat that the Hallins and Lees had not joined Help, Inc. No autopsies were performed on any of the three animals. "There wasn't any need to."

Late Saturday afternoon Brother Wilson had come to take Jan to Jackson to spend the weekend with the Don Jacksons before going on to Forest. It was now apparent that she was far more serious about him than about any of the other young men she had been dating.

When the Heffners had supper later Sunday night with Leon and Joan Pickard in Magnolia, they were astounded to hear that there was a military force of some thirty helmeted men drilling regularly every Thursday night on the courthouse lawn. It seemed so futile to the Heffners. Were they preparing to fight college boys, the local Negroes, or the full force of the United States government?

The week beginning on Monday, August 31, was for the Heffners the most crowded and fateful of the summer.

It started quietly enough. Lyda Will and Oliver telephoned just to find out if they were all right. Red drove to Poplarville, seventy-five miles away, to present to Movie Star, Inc., manufacturers of ladies' lingerie, a revised group hospitalization proposal. It was all so natural.

But because of the harassment calls and the hard economic facts of life, there seemed to be no future for them in McComb. Still they hated to make the break.

Nostalgically, Red and Malva walked around their yard a lot these days examining the pines they had planted, the banana trees which drooped over the patio, the azaleas, more than 150 of them, against the house and in the beds on the property line. In their first fall in Mc-Comb, Red and Jan had put out a young magnolia tree with three leaves. Now it was over twelve feet tall, perfectly shaped, healthy and luxuriant.

If the family was going to move to Jackson, the move should be made before school started. This was Carla's senior year. Naturally she had expected to share with her friends in the senior activities to which she had looked forward throughout high school. But if staying in Mc-Comb was going to be impossible, she wanted to matriculate at a Jackson high school in time to start with her class. No final decision about moving had been made. However, it seemed wise to the family that they look for a place to live in Jackson.

Wednesday Malva and Carla left early for Jackson. When they came back the next day they reported that they had found nothing that came up to their own home. However, there was one apartment house, the Jefferson Place, that had some attractive features.

Carla liked its swimming pool and its inclusion in the Murrah High School district, which she had been told offered the most stimulating courses in the city's school system. Malva said that the wall around the building and the locked gates with a key for each tenant and an electric release from the apartment would make her feel more secure than she had in a long time. But no firm commitment had been made to the apartment resident manager.

While they were gone, Red had received an encouraging letter from LeRoy Collins, director of the newly established Federal Community Relations Service, and important papers which moved the Gulf States Theatre's pension plan closer to installation. A friend telephoned from Greenville to express her concern. She said she had heard all sorts of terrible rumors and their Greenville friends were worried. Only word-of-mouth versions had circulated because, true to their promises, the newsmen who knew the story were still holding it.

Thursday night something happened that settled the question of leaving McComb and moving quietly to Jackson.

Carla took the Chevy II and picked up four of her friends to go by to see Sarah Smith, one of their schoolmates, who had just returned from the hospital. Before Carla left the house, Malva told her that, for safety's sake, she wanted her back in the house no later than ten o'clock. She surprised the family by coming home earlier and frightened. She told her parents that when she and the girls walked out of Sarah's, they had found all four tires flat. Someone had let the air out. She hadn't realized that theirs was a marked car and this could happen to her. Carla told her parents she understood now what they had been going through.

In the morning Red went to the bank and borrowed money they would need to move. They would go during the following week.

But over Labor Day weekend a chain of related events made earning a living as an insurance agent in Jackson or probably anywhere else in the state an impossibility.

At about five-thirty Friday afternoon a man who identified himself as Frank Nussbaum telephoned from the Holiday Inn. He was a friend of Jonah, whom he had met two years before when as a Fulbright Scholar he had lived in Jonah's dormitory at the Free University of Berlin. He had called Jonah from Chicago to say that he and two friends would like to see him while they were touring the Deep South. Jonah told him that he was leaving the next day, but to get in touch with the Heffners when he reached town. Nussbaum identified himself as being from Rockford, Illinois, and a candidate for a Ph.D. in mathematics at Northwestern University. With him were another mathematics postgraduate student, George Chrones of Eugene, Oregon, and a German, Joachim Fechner, a director of youth welfare work in the Steglitz District of Berlin. Fechner had come to the States for six months under a Fulbright travel grant and the Cleveland, Ohio, International Program, which arranges an exchange of international social workers.

Red told Nussbaum that he would drive right over and lead them to his house. They were completely unassociated with civil rights activities and it didn't occur to him to recommend that they leave their car at the Inn. Red admits that these travelers and their automobile added up to a "pretty raunchy-looking lot." The three men had been squeezed into a Volkswagen with a good deal of luggage for hours of driving on a hot summer day. The two Americans wore road-weary Bermuda shorts. The forty-year-old German sported the Bavarian lederhosen and three-quarter stockings. The Volkswagen had a

heavily laden luggage rack and an Illinois license. In Mc-
Comb they were licked before they started.

At the house Frank Nussbaum told more about his connection with Joachim Fechner, whom he called Jim. When
he first went to Germany, he had lived for a while with
the Fechner family, mother, father, and three young sons.
He also told how they had decided to come to Mississippi.

"I had written Jonah earlier in the summer and told of
our plans to visit Mississippi. In Berlin he had invited me
to visit him in Magnolia. But when I wrote from Illinois,
his answer seemed mysterious to me. He indicated he
was under pressure to leave town because of involvement
in civil rights. The letter was full of hints, but explained
very little. He said he was afraid to explain in writing.

"The letter reminded Jim very much of the type letter
he exchanges with his relatives in East Germany, and it
reminded my mother of the type letter she received from
her relatives in Hitlerite Germany. I called Jonah, only
to find out we would miss him by several days. But he
did give me your name and address and urged us to
visit you. The phone call was even more mysterious than
the letter. I could tell Jonah would have liked to tell me
what was going on, but he didn't dare. Anyway, all this
heightened our sense of anticipation.

"But then we got cold feet because of the advice given
us by many people, some of them Southerners, and because of the Philadelphia killings. We decided to avoid
Mississippi on our Southern tour. Then in Memphis we
asked the advice of a Negro policeman who told us we
wouldn't get into trouble as long as we didn't travel

113

mixed. Only then did we change our minds. So that brings us to the Holiday Inn."

After an introductory half hour or so, Red suggested that Fechner might be interested in reading the bylaws and instructions put out by Help, Inc., a copy of which had been given to him by Jim Millstone.

"I have never seen such a change come over anyone," Red says. "He had just said that the rules reminded him of Germany under Hitler when Jan and Brother Wilson came in. They took one look at our three guests and must have concluded that they were somewhat older COFO workers. Their faces were something to see. While I was introducing and trying to identify our guests, the telephone rang. It was Helen Hallin across the street. She told Malva that automobiles were circling the house again and that Pete was trailing them in his own car to try to discover who the occupants were. Helen was giving a party at the time for her eleven-year-old daughter, Debbie, and understandably she was getting nervous herself because she was afraid the children might get upset. A little while later mothers started picking up their children. The party was breaking up early because word had already gotten around that the Heffners were under surveillance again and that anything might happen."

Helen Hallin's telephone call touched off something in Brother Wilson. He announced angrily that he was leaving. To the disquiet of her parents, Jan said that she would go with him. "It was her decision and I told her that I would make no effort to get her to stay," Red relates. "It was a tremendously sad moment in the midst of chaos and confusion. After they left the rest of us agreed that the three visitors should also leave."

Red telephoned the police and asked that a patrol car follow the strangers out of town to the Louisiana state line. The memory of the Philadelphia victims was fresh and frightening, for the bodies had been found only twenty-seven days before.

A police car arrived soon thereafter and stopped in the middle of the street. Helen Hallin came out and protested vigorously to the two policemen about a state of mind which required guests to be escorted out of the city and the state for their own safety. The police apparently thought it funny. Their only response was to laugh. But they dutifully followed the Volkswagen with the Illinois license when Nussbaum, Chrones, and Fechner drove off to the sanity of the Louisiana line. Somewhat later in the evening the FBI, interested especially because of the German national in the car, checked with the state highway patrol and learned that the three were well into Louisiana.

The rest of the incident is best told in the words of Joachim Fechner, who wrote at least twice to American friends. One letter was to the Heffners personally, the other was a mimeographed recital which went to all the friends he had made in the United States. In this he wrote:

"Far out of town the police convoy stopped us on the highway and one of the policemen explained the whole incident to us. It was a real long speech, though only a few extracts: 'I don't want you to leave with a bad taste in your mouths,' he said, 'but there was no reason to be scared or worried. We have been informed about your visit long before your host called us. All the people around the house wouldn't hurt you, they had been there to protect and to watch you that nothing happens to you. We have our Southern way of life and it always works excellent. Everybody was content and happy. The niggers too don't want to change. But then the agitators from the North came and stirred our niggers up. Awful things happened. These COFO people came down and even were staying in the niggers' homes. I am here to enforce the law. Now the new civil rights law has been passed. But there are some parts that just don't go along with me. I grew up and was taught not to wet my bed. All the time I got up in the night and used the washroom. Now such a guy comes along and tells you: it's O.K. to piss in your bed. Say, what would you do, would you piss in your bed? The niggers here are quite different from the North: they are purple-lipped, flat-nosed, knotheaded, scrawny bastards that smell like a goat. We are all equal, but in different classes. I hope you don't leave us with a bad taste in your mouth.'"

A few days later, when the two Americans and the German drove from New Orleans to the Mississippi Gulf Coast, they were picked up in Gulfport and held in a barred room for an hour; the excuse of the police was that Fechner's identity and papers had to be checked. They were then questioned by a civilian, obviously a detective, who wanted only to know why they were in Mississippi at all. At the end of the interrogation he said that they were free to go but warned them to leave the state because of an approaching hurricane.

In Fechner's lengthy letter to the Heffners he told them in labored English what life was like under the Nazis and of his own activities as an underground opponent of the party at the age of seventeen. Here is one paragraph which certainly belongs in this story:

"I feel very sad about all the worse things that have happened to you and I wish to assure you my sympathy and my deep feelings for you. There might be not much chance for me but if I can help you anyhow, please let me know. We shouldn't have driven down to your house, I really feel guilty about doing this visit and I feel shamed that I haven't prohibited this visit that ought to endanger you; nobody should have known it better than myself, since none of you have the experiences in this special field as a German unfortunately has. The only excuse I can give is that I never had believed that things are really this bad. It is somewhat similar to the experiences during the Nazi time, when you heard sometimes rumors about concentration camps and persecutions, but never really believed or took it serious enough. So actually I didn't learn my lesson as yet and there is no excuse. Please forgive me and all of us for the harm we did to you."

Malva had been near the breaking point for weeks.

The door had hardly closed on the last visitor they would have in McComb when she blew her top. If a family couldn't entertain a foreign visitor and a couple of non-Southern Americans in McComb, Mississippi, without coming under surveillance of a bunch of vigilantes the state was in a mess. She tried to reach Governor Johnson by telephone to demand that he do something to restore law and order and sanity in the state. The governor was out of pocket and the aide to whom Malva spoke her mind with certain embellishments took evasive action.

It was then that the Heffners said a final to-hell-with-it.

Already Jim Millstone of the St. Louis *Post-Dispatch* and Nick Von Hoffman of the Chicago *Daily News* had their own stories ready. With an odd sort of continuing loyalty to their state, Red and Malva now thought that they should let the states' newspapers have the story first. Malva telephoned the Emmerichs to tell them of the decision. Lyda Will urged her not to go through with it, warning her that it would do no good, reminding her that when Oliver was slugged the story was widely circulated and that, although there were witnesses, the attacker went free. The reporter who answered her at the Jackson *Clarion-Ledger*, the state's largest and possibly worst newspaper, showed no interest whatsoever in the story. She then telephoned Hodding Carter, III, managing editor of the Delta *Democrat-Times*, Greenville. He was out of town, but a reporter interviewed her for more than an hour. The next calls were made to Jim Millstone and Nick Von Hoffman, whom they told to go ahead if they wished to. Malva then telephoned the Associated Press and United Press International in Jackson. The AP man suggested that she set up a press conference. Neither Red nor Malva knew how to arrange a press conference. Malva phoned COFO headquarters and whoever answered said that it would be attended to. Here was the point of no return. The people of McComb would

118

remember only that the press conference made their town look bad and that the freedom workers had arranged the conference at which Malva changed what they thought was their town's pleasant image. There was to be a mass forgetfulness that the burning and bombing of Negro churches and homes might also have had something to do with the changed image.

Malva and Red and Carla packed their personal belongings. Jan by now had taken refuge at the Wilsons' in Rosedale.

Early in the morning Nick, who had been in Natchez the night before, and a Chicago *Daily News* photographer, Henry Gill, arrived. They had had a bad night, too. After trying to cover a civil rights meeting in Adams County, they had been followed to their motel by patrolmen. Officers and police dogs surrounded them until the FBI arrived to investigate.

"I rented a U-Haul trailer," Red says. "Nick and Henry helped us load it with all the impractical but cherished things a family accumulates, scrapbooks, pictures, trophies. We got a call from Jim Millstone for a few confirming details. We also gave a story for the New York papers to Ellis Bert, one of the civil rights lawyers. And then I told George Guy that all of this was going to break in the papers.

"Malva went ahead to Jackson with Mitch Thomas, a young friend from Summit, in his car. The press conference had been set for two o'clock at the Sun 'N Sand Motel in Jackson and I doubted that I would get there in time. Carla followed her mother in the Impala, with

119

her parakeet as her traveling companion. Malva didn't want her at the press conference, so she went straight to the apartment. By the time the trailer had been loaded I knew that I could not make it either. But that was all right because I knew Malva could handle it."

Nick and Henry, who had been helping Red load and knew the story anyway, followed Red to the apartment.

What happened at the press conference is Malva's story:

"When Mitch and I arrived at the Sun 'N Sand, there were newsmen setting up TV cameras and more men coming in—not a face was familiar—and I was scared and sick with bitterness and hurt. When James Jones of UPI and formerly from McComb walked in and put his arms around me, I started crying because of his kindness. Questions were being thrown at me from all around, which made answering difficult. How could anyone explain in a few sentences what had happened to us? I was told I only had five minutes by WLBT because of a lack of film. Dennis Sweeney walked in and he was the second familiar face. We embraced and this was later to be used in the Jackson papers to smear me. No mention was ever made of the hug by James Jones, only Dennis, the SNCC worker at McComb.

"The Jackson papers and TV stations didn't want this story. It was never really told in detail and Mississippi people only knew the truth through a few Mississippi papers and out-of-state news media. The *Enterprise-Journal* in McComb carried the St. Louis *Post-Dispatch* story by Jim Millstone."

The *Enterprise-Journal* carried its own story sooner than that, though. It read in part:

"Mr. and Mrs. Heffner, parents of Jan Nave, Miss Mississippi of 1963, hit the headlines Sunday after a Saturday news conference during which Mrs. Heffner said her family was forced to leave McComb.

"She said her home at 202 Shannon Dr. was beset by a flood of threatening or obscene telephone calls, three pets were killed and she feared the home would be bombed.

"The trouble started after white civil rights workers in McComb visited the Heffner residence in July, and many of the neighbors became upset about it.

"After rumors spread throughout the city about the visit, Heffner made a statement in the *Enterprise-Journal* on July 22 in which he said he invited the workers to his home to tell them the Mississippi point of view.

MENTIONS HELP

"A Council of Federated Organizations worker, Dennis Sweeney, was at Mrs. Heffner's Jackson press conference Saturday. He and the Rev. Don McCord were reportedly the COFO workers who visited the Heffners.

"At the press conference, Mrs. Heffner called Help, Inc., a community organization composed of residents of Carroll Oaks and Westview Circle, a 'fear clique.'

"An officer of Help, Inc., contacted by the *Enterprise-Journal* today, said the organization would have no comment on Mrs. Heffner's charges at this time.

"Officials of Help, Inc., which recently held a community-wide pot-luck supper, have previously

121

stated the organization is solely for the purpose of enabling neighbors to get to know and help each other.

CHARGES MAYOR

"Mrs. Heffner also charged Mayor Gordon Burt condoned the activities of the organization.

"Mayor Burt said in his office this morning that he hasn't necessarily condoned the group because he wasn't thoroughly familiar with all of its aims. He said he hadn't been asked to condone its actions.

"He did, the mayor noted, speak at a neighborhood meeting called by the group, but did so at their invitation and he explained his position of not welcoming civil rights workers to McComb and left before any other business was transacted.

BURT'S SIDE

"Burt claimed that, insofar as he knows, the Heffners never asked the city for any help to stop the reported threats.

"'They are apparently on better terms with COFO than they are with the city,' he said.

"'Apparently Mrs. Heffner and I have different attitudes about COFO. I can assure you Mr. Sweeney would not embrace me.'"

CHAPTER VIII

The furnished Jefferson Place apartment on the south-west corner of the second floor was clean and modern, though the rooms seemed small after the home in Carroll Oaks. Red paid a month's rent in advance, soon after he arrived with the laden U-Haul trailer. He, Nick, Henry, and Carla had started unloading by the time Malva and Mitch Thomas arrived from the press conference. They all carried the miscellany of household goods up to the apartment and began trying to make it something like a home.

Carla had a date that night and Nick Von Hoffman invited Red and Malva to dinner at Le Fleur's with Henry Gill and himself. He had wanted to take them to the Rotisserie, his favorite Jackson restaurant, but the last time he had gone there he found that the Rotisserie, like many another Southern eating place, had become a private club. The manager declined to give him a membership card because of articles he had written which were less than complimentary to the state.

The evening was not festive. Red and Malva were

greatly disturbed over Nick's disclosure that he and Henry were going back to Southwest Mississippi, the most dangerous region in the state for outsiders and up-pity Negroes, to interview Ku Klux Klan members who might be willing to talk. Nick had a different concern. The four had heard Malva's taped interview on the radio just before going out and Nick said bluntly that while the story had to be told he was afraid they'd had it. The Heffners were more sanguine. Malva said that there were more fair-minded people in the Jackson area than Nick might think. Red could still make a decent living selling insurance, he said. He was a good salesman.

Before Red went to bed he made a brief entry in his diary: "The fat is in the fire but, damnit all, we tried."

The next morning Red drove the Chevy II to McComb with Nick as a passenger. Henry Gill drove Nick's car. Red and Malva had forgotten the table silver and there was a good automobile load of other belongings that they could use. Nick had arranged to interview Mayor Burt. Neither Malva nor Carla came along.

The still-taut Malva needed rest and Carla had the Jefferson Place swimming pool on her mind. On the way out Red stopped at the apartment-house office to use the telephone and Mr. Griffin, the manager, observed casually that he didn't know how the other tenants were going to react to the press conference. Red, with a sinking feeling in his stomach, said that he thought everything would turn out all right.

Red had one good laugh on the way back from Mc-Comb. Mayor Burt had told Nick during his interview that the Heffners were "guilty of a breach of etiquette when they admitted Dennis Sweeney and Don McCord into their home." With the mayor during Nick's interview were two vice-presidents of Help, Inc.

They reached the Jefferson Place late in the afternoon and went up to the apartment, each carrying an armload of belongings. They were not prepared for what Malva had to tell them.

Early that afternoon, she said, Carla had put on her bathing suit and gone downstairs to the pool. At about the same time Father Duncan Hobart, rector of St. James' Episcopal Church, had come by to offer his services to the family which, after reading the morning newspaper, he knew to be in trouble.

Carla came back almost immediately, saying that as she walked past the manager's office Mrs. Griffin had asked her to tell Malva that the manager wished to see her. Carla left again for the pool.

"All I could think was here we go again. And I felt as if I were going to faint," Malva remembers. "Father Hobart suggested that I go downstairs and see the manager while he was still with me."

So Malva went down to the Griffin apartment.

"Mr. Griffin asked me where Red was. I told him, 'In McComb.' Then he said, 'You'll have to leave the apartment tomorrow.' I answered that we would. As I left the room Mrs. Griffin, who had kept her head down while her husband was talking, said in a low voice, 'I'm very sorry, Mrs. Heffner.' I started crying as I answered, 'The closed society is still closing in.' Then I hurried out of the room. I think God had something to do with Father Hobart being with me at the apartment."

Duncan Hobart, a gentle, resolute idealist, comforted her as best he could and made a thoughtful offer. He and his wife were going on vacation the next day. The Heffners must stay in the rectory until they could find another place. There was plenty of storage room for their things, he said, and no one would bother them there. If anyone dropped by, it would only be friendly neighbors wondering who was occupying the rectory while the Hobarts were away.

Within minutes Mrs. Hobart was showing Malva around the rectory, so that she would know where everything was.

Malva wanted to stop by and tell the Auburn Lambeths what had developed, so Father Hobart drove her to the Lambeths' home and, after she had eaten a dish of ice cream, the Lambeths brought her back to the Jefferson Place.

Red cursed some in anger as she told what had happened. But there was nothing for it but to move.

A Labor Day is no time to find a trailer or packing boxes to replace those which had been disposed of Saturday evening. But Red managed and by noon he and Nick and Henry were loading up again. At about this time another Episcopal priest, Father Alex Dickson, of St. Columb's, appeared. He had not heard of their eviction but knew they had left McComb and just happened to call. He pitched in and helped load the trailer. More important, he was the only one of the group who knew how to back a trailer, and did.

Before the loading was done, the Reverend Jack Biggers, assistant to Father Hobart, came in. He suggested
that it might be better not to get St. James' Parish involved as it would be if the rectory, which was church
property, housed the Heffners. He offered to let the
family use his apartment at the Magnolia Towers and
said that he would move into the rectory while they were
in his place. At his apartment they might feel even more
shielded from the public than at the Hobarts', he pointed
out.

The Heffners acquiesced. They were emotionally
drained. The problem of what to do with their twin beds
and other furniture they had moved from McComb to
give a homier look to their apartment, and for which
Father Biggers' one-bedroom efficiency apartment would
have no space, seemed insurmountable. Auburn Lambeth
offered to let them store the furniture and household
utensils temporarily in his garage.

Labor Day afternoon Red and Malva and Carla moved
to the Magnolia Towers. There was no certainty left in
life. Where they would go from there, what they would
do, were all part of a great terrifying question: What
comes after you've had it?

"At this point Malva and I are in a state of shock and
don't know which way to turn," Red wrote in his diary.
"Bishop Allin is out of town. Called Bishop Moore in
Washington about some sort of help in getting Carla in
school. Malva is beginning to break. She is crying every
night. Jan and Brother came by to get a key to the
house. She needed to get out her clothes for school. They
stayed only a few minutes."

127

The Heffners' immediate concern still was the problem of Carla's schooling. Friday morning she had picked up her schedule along with the other seniors at McComb High School, knowing that it was a vain gesture. The Jackson school system was to commence classes a week from Labor Day. If the family was not going to be able to remain in Jackson, other arrangements for her schooling would have to be made. "I'm not a high school dropout. I'm a force-out," Carla quipped.

Red telephoned Bishop Allin Tuesday. The bishop offered to write a letter to St. Mary's at Sewanee, Tennessee, and told Red he could use his name when he called the school himself, but the school offered little encouragement so late in the season.

That same day Red was dealt another blow. Auburn Lambeth, who had done the best he could, told him that he had spoken to the Lincoln National home office in Fort Wayne and reported that the executive vice-president and the vice-president in charge of sales thought that Red was too old to be moved to another area and it would not be in his best interest. As Red and Lambeth had already decided that it would be unwise for Red to be identified with the Jackson office, Red knew he was through. "I did not think I could get much lower than yesterday but I have," Red noted.

CHAPTER IX

Help came out of the blue. Yet another Episcopal priest gave aid and comfort.

The Reverend Warren McKenna of Massachusetts was in Jackson in early September as a representative of the National Council of Churches. Nick Von Hoffman, who knew McKenna and was still in Jackson, told McKenna that the Episcopal Church ought to do something for a man who was trying to practice what the church preached. McKenna was at the Sun 'N Sand with his wife, who had just arrived from Boston.

Father McKenna carried through. After meeting the Heffners, he telephoned the Episcopal Center in New York City, the office of the Right Reverend Arthur Lichtenberger, Presiding Bishop of the Episcopal Church. On Bishop Lichtenberger's instructions, the Reverend Arthur E. Walmsley, executive secretary of the Division of Christian Citizenship of the Department of Christian Social Relations of the Church, took charge.

What Red didn't enter in his diary was that he was fast becoming as distraught as his wife. He had written or telephoned almost everyone he thought could help him and other calls had been made on his behalf to people throughout the government.

"The one light that shone in our darkness was the concern and kindness of the Episcopal clergy," Red says.

Father Walmsley telephoned from New York Thursday morning. He had arranged for the Heffners to fly to New York the next day. Tickets for Red and Malva and Carla would be waiting at the airport.

Red drove again to McComb to pick up clothes for the journey. At last something was happening that couldn't be bad.

Red still can't believe that anyone could be as kind as were new and old friends in New York. The Episcopal Church had reserved a small suite for them at the Beekman Towers. Ben and Muriel Sokobin, with whom Carla had spent the summer, met them at the Newark Airport. Dr. Levin, the psychologist, had flowers for the ladies and a gift package for Red waiting in the room at the hotel.

At the Episcopal Center to which they went directly from the airport, Bishop Lichtenberger listened intently to their story and said reassuringly that the Church would at least be able to do something.

Immediately a task force of churchmen and friends began to work on finding a school for Carla. Bishop Moore telephoned Carroll Greene, an associate secretary of the Division of Christian Citizenship, to say that there was a near-miraculous vacancy at the National Cathedral School for Girls in Washington. Greene began working on the financing which would be required above a small scholarship and the following Wednesday Malva took Carla to Washington and entered her in the school.

During their ten days in New York, friends entertained the Heffners at home and in well-known restaurants. The granddaughter of a former Mississippi governor offered them the use of her home. Jack Ryan, who came from Summit and had spent the past nine Christmas Eves with the Heffners in McComb, gave them moral support. It was good to see Father Harry Bowie again. But an incident at dinner one night in a suburban New York town recorded in Red's diary brought home that prejudice is not a Mississippi monopoly. "The most amazing thing of the evening," he noted. "The area where we had dinner is about sixty-five per cent Jewish. A former president of the local B'Nai B'Rith chapter has circulated a petition against a Chinese family moving into the neighborhood. It is a warm and wonderful neighborhood and far better than this crackpot."

With Carla established in school, the remaining and major problem was what Red would do. Because their daughter would be in Washington, the Heffners decided they would prefer to make that area home. So they went there in search of a job for Red.

In the latter part of the month Malva flew back to Mississippi. She knew that the Hobarts would be coming home and Father Biggers would want the Heffners' things to have been moved out of his little apartment before he returned to it. Father McKenna met her at the plane and took her to the King Edward Hotel, where she picked up her car which had been stored there.

After filling a number of boxes at the Magnolia Towers

131

apartment, she left early in the morning for McComb, thinking she could stay with the Colton Smiths during the two days it would take her to close the house. But they were on the Gulf Coast at a church conference, as was Libby Price, and the town of McComb was in unparalleled turmoil.

During the month of September the number of bombings had rapidly increased and by the end of the month the police-harassment arrests of the COFO workers were becoming acute. Dennis had been arrested twice in two days. Sixteen workers were put into jail on charges of criminal syndicalism, under a bill passed in Governor Paul Johnson's first session of the legislature. Under this law it is a criminal offense to advocate change in the political or social structure of the state. Burgland, the Negro section of McComb east of the Illinois Central track, was near riot. Every car entering or leaving it was being checked.

Malva went to Helen Hallin's to see her and to use the telephone. When Malva called the Holiday Inn she learned Harry Raddon was in Memphis and the clerk said there was no room available. Helen warned Malva that she did not think it would be safe for her to remain in McComb after dark.

If was under these conditions of terror that she hastily assembled what she could and left for her mother's. Even there, family and friends could not understand or accept Malva's and Red's concern about the lives and safety of the hated and despised COFO outsiders.

After mailing Carla several boxes of clothes from Forest, Malva went to Red's parents' at Greenwood.

While she was there, he telephoned her the encouraging news that he had been retained as a pension consultant for the AFL-CIO for a six weeks' period. After that he would become associated with a new life insurance company, the Variable Annuity Life Insurance Company of America. Now she would have to return to McComb to complete arrangements for the move. She felt a little more comfortable about going back to McComb. On September 30 three white Pike County men accused of arson or bombing had been arrested.

Inside the house with the for-sale sign on the front lawn she sorted and prepared everything for the van. Her maid, Essie Martin, helped her late into the night, though Malva reminded her that, while the Heffners were leaving, she would be staying. When Malva was exhausted she went to the Colton Smiths' to spend the night. Again there had been no room at the Holiday Inn. Hurricane Hilda had brought many refugees up from the Coast.

By the second night she had done all she could. Pete Hallin helped tape the boxes and took down the draperies. After dark, in the heavy driving rain which came with the hurricane's backlash, she was driven to Jackson by a SNCC worker and a minister from Freedom House. Red met her at the Sun 'N Sand, from where they started for Washington in their two heavily loaded automobiles.

Before leaving the state, on October 8, they drove through Columbus to tell Jan goodbye at M.S.C.W. They had been worried by a news release put out by the college to the effect that while Jan loved her parents she did not agree with them. This was the saddest part. They were leaving their home and all they had and their daughter in Mississippi.

CHAPTER X

It is unlikely that during the dreadful summer any of McComb's white ministers other than Colton Smith pointed publicly to the cross of Christ in rebuke or even in reminder. The surest indication that none did is that all of them are still there when the collection plates are passed. In fairness one must observe that few are the Protestant shepherds anywhere who relish being butted by their flock into a lean martyrdom overnight.

But if the sign of the cross was unavailing at the beginning or the end of the summer, another sign, the dollar sign, was not. Whatever McComb's citizens thought of themselves or their town in November 1964, few had any illusions about how most of their fellow Americans regarded them. The very name of McComb was a hissing. The community stood little chance of adding a payroll in the ascertainable future, certainly not until the beatings, the defiance of law, the bombings, the individual persecutions had abated. Business was at its lowest ebb since before World War II. Too many housewives were nervous about going downtown on leisurely shopping expeditions and too many Negroes were either doing without or driving across the Louisiana line to make their purchases.

The dollar sign was backed by the twin virtues of community pride and community conscience.

In the latter part of September, when racial incidents had become part of the daily pattern of life, Sheriff Warren came into the *Enterprise-Journal* office and told Oliver that he thought he could bring them to an end quickly if he only had some reward money with which to pay for information as to the identity of the bombers. The Board of Supervisors of the county and the city government had turned down his request. The $3000 he said he needed seemed a reasonable amount to raise in the interest of law and order.

Here at last was a new factor in the anarchical situation which had prevailed so long. Oliver saw something to tie to after four lonely months.

It may be that when he addressed himself in September to the subject of lawlessness, his eyes were figuratively bleared from the intrusion of rising smoke, his nose afflicted by the acrid stench of black gunpowder, his civic loyalty and pride shaken by uncivil barbarism, and his soul tormented by the question: What ever happened to the Lord Jesus Christ in McComb?

His front-page editorial asking for donations to a reward fund was more effective than the editorials back in May. To his surprise the appeal brought in more than $5000 over the weekend. One week later the first three suspects were arrested. In the next few days eight others were also charged with bombings.

The arrests had a curious outcome. Judge William A. Watkins, Jr., the circuit court jurist in whose front yard a cross had been burned earlier in the summer, placed on probation the eleven men who admitted or declined to contest the accusations with a warning that they would go to jail if there were any more bombings. The judge's defenders said, with considerable justification, that had the men been tried by a Pike County jury they would have gone free and might also have gone far in county politics, that is, all culprits save one. This worthy did not go scot-free as he was arrested soon thereafter and charged with the holdup of a near-by rural bank.

Finding in the support of the September editorial a solid foundation beneath the turbulent hysteria of the past few months, Oliver began running a hard-hitting series of editorials. For over a month he used every argument he could think of to bring the community back to a recognition that compliance with the civil rights law, unpopular though that law might be, was the only way out of the community's dilemma.

The first of these editorials, on October 14, summed up "the sordid story of McComb" which, the editor said, was not something to be brushed aside as being the handiwork of "a hostile, out-of-state press." The situation demanded responsible thinking, a willingness by each person to analyze his or her own attitude toward law and order, for, he wrote, many must share in the responsibility for violence, even though they may not have been near the scenes of violence. The *Enterprise-Journal* appealed for "an intensive spiritual drive to establish responsible thinking and action."

After thirteen editorials he was able to report that the City Board of Mayor and Selectmen had voted that in the future no harassment arrests would be made without the unanimous approval of the police committee of the City Board. Heartened by this, Oliver stated the issue squarely in his editorial of November 3:

> The first step toward community responsibility in McComb is the public will to restore law and order to the point where every citizen has the assurance of protection.
>
> The second step of responsible men and women must be to uphold the laws governing voter registration.

The immediate response to this editorial was a bullet through the newspaper's plate-glass window.

Undeterred, the editor recommenced his crusade for responsible action six days later.

While the series of editorials was appearing, a self-constituted committee of four men of impeccable community standing, among them the editor, was studying what could be done to re-establish law and order in McComb. It quickly grew to be a committee of twenty and then of fifty-one. And the yeast of reason began to leaven the body politic. Dr. Ralph L. Brock, president of the McComb Rotary Club, wrote a letter to the editor suggesting that Rotary's 4-Way Test be applied to what was happening in the town; the County Board of Supervisors passed a resolution condemning violence, violation of law, intimidation, threats, and coercion by and to any

138

and all citizens of Pike County; and the Magnolia Chamber of Commerce urged the county citizens to maintain allegiance to law and order.

Meanwhile, the committee had drawn up a Statement of Principles to which it obtained an initial 650 signatures. Many others were added later. The declaration, with the signatures, was published as a full-page advertisement in the *Enterprise-Journal* on November 17 and as part of a commendatory editorial the next day. The declaration, which no public officials or employees were asked to sign, though some did sign voluntarily, read:

> The great majority of our citizens believe in law and order and are against violence of any kind. In spite of this, acts of terrorism have been committed numerous times against citizens both Negro and white.
>
> We believe the time has come for responsible people to speak out for what is right and against what is wrong. For too long we have let the extremists on both sides bring our community close to chaos.
>
> There is only one responsible stance we can take: and that is for equal treatment under the law for all citizens regardless of race, creed, position or wealth; for making our protests within the framework of the law; and for obeying the laws of the land regardless of our personal feelings. Certain of these laws may be contrary to our traditions, customs or beliefs, but as God-fearing men and women, and as citizens of these United States, we see no other honorable course to follow.
>
> To these ends and for the purpose of restoring

139

peace, tranquility and progress to our area, we respectfully urge the following:

1. Order and respect for law must be re-established and maintained.

(a) Law officers should make only lawful arrests. "Harassment" arrests, no matter what the provocation, are not consonant with impartiality of the law.

(b) To insure the confidence of the people in their officials, we insist that no man is entitled to serve in a public office, elective or appointive, who is a member of any organization declared to be subversive by the Senate Internal Security Sub-Committee or the United States Army, Navy or Air Force, or to take any obligation upon himself in conflict with his oath of office.

2. Economic threats and sanctions against people of both races must be ended. They only bring harm to both races.

3. We urge citizens of both races to re-establish avenues of communication and understanding. In addition, it is urged that the Negro leadership cooperate with local officials.

4. We urge widest possible use of our citizenship in the selection of juries. We further urge that men called for jury duty not be excused except for the most compelling reasons.

5. We urge our fellow citizens to take a greater interest in public affairs, in the selection of candidates, and in the support and/or constructive criticism of Public Servants.

6. We urge all of our people to approach the future with a renewed dedication and to reflect an attitude of optimism about our county.

These objectives were all that Red and Malva had wanted to achieve from the beginning, when, just four months earlier to the day, they sat down before a platter of hot tamales with two civil rights workers in their home.

The day after the statement was published, the Holiday Inn, which turned away Malva Heffner when she came back to McComb in September, welcomed, in a manner of speaking, two Negro guests. State highway police, patrolmen, and deputies made up the welcoming committee.

Oliver was able to report with satisfaction that the civic image of McComb was already greatly improved and that radio, television, columnists, and news magazines were helping in projecting the happier spectacle of a community complying with the law.

Soon afterward, Oliver telephoned Drew Pearson, who had written a caustic column about the hounding of the Heffners. The editor asked the Washington columnist if he could find someone who could persuade the COFO people to leave McComb and thus further help the situation. Pearson passed the request on to Red. "There's only one approach," Red told Pearson. "We've got to go along with the civil rights program all the way. All down the line. That's the only way to get the COFOs out of McComb, short of killing them."

It would be pleasant to end with praise for a community's catharsis. But although brighter days may lie ahead for Pike County, there may yet be other flame-bright nights. To the tom-tom accompaniment of the Magnolia *Gazette* and the Summit *Sun*, three counter-petitions were circulated. They were later combined into one and the total number of signatures endorsing them was some 1200, about 200 more than the number of citizens who from first to last signed the original statement for law and order.

A last family note or so. Jan and Brother Wilson were married in the First Methodist Church in Forest by an Episcopal priest on the day after Christmas. They are living in Jackson where, by coincidence, Brother is associated with an insurance company. Red, Malva, and Carla attended the wedding. Red gave the bride away and Carla, who wanted to call this account of the family's fortunes "Nobody Gave a Damn," was maid of honor. Only one adult couple came over from McComb, but a good many of Jan and Carla's friends did.

Red and Malva would like to come home to Mississippi some day, but not to McComb. In May, Red became a conciliator with the Community Relations Service, a position he had sought when the Heffners first moved to Washington, and Malva a field worker for Operation Headstart in the Office of Economic Opportunity. They have found a purchaser for the little flat-top house that was the first to be built in Carroll Oaks and in whose backyard is buried a lovable dachshund named Falstaff.

CPSIA information can be obtained at www.ICGtesting.com
Printed in the USA
BVOW08s0030230316

441401BV00001B/2/P